50 quirky bike rides

for family and friends,

free from *freightlining*

juggernauts and white van

road **rage**, in eco friendly, carbon neutral, NATURALLY *blissful*, THRILLS and hills, on a hunch over *lunch*, with w!nks over *drinks*, brooks beckon, waves *lap*, *wind* whizzes - the most *thrilling* downhilling and app⊂ealing freewheeling, on trains, **bridges**, p l a i n s & ridges the odD, *unique*, *eccentric* and curious, from *flying* canals to haunted tunnels to underwater roads the *longest, prettiest, bendiest, bounciest, rockiest, twistiest, zingiest, peakiest, prettiest, whizziest, bestest,*

bestest *BESTEST*

bike rides

in England and Wales *(ever)*

by Rob Ainsley

KU-348-946

BIZARRE BIKING

50 Quirky Bike Rides...in England and Wales
1st Edition
June 2008

Published by Eye Books Ltd
8 Peacock Yard
London
SE17 3LH
Tel: +44 (0) 845 450 8870
website: www.eye-books.com

Typeset in ITC Officina, Berling and Rotis sans serif
ISBN: 978 1903070550
ISBN: 1 9030705 54

British Library Cataloguing in Publication Data
A catalogue record for this book is available from the British Library

Photographss by the author, except for some public domain images used in the postcards, and the following:

Clay Trails p 26-29: J Bewley and Dave Cuffwright, Sustrans
Eynsford p49 (left): Chris Jones
Dunwich Dynamo p102-105: Simon Nuttall
Crap Cycle Lanes p200: Warrington Cycle Campaign

Design by David Whelan for Eye Books

Introduction

This is a bike book with a difference. It's not a catalogue of routes. It's not a travelogue. It's not a history of the Tour de France.

It's a description of and guide to 50 quirky places in England and Wales that are uniquely enjoyable by bike. The most spectacular bridges; the best tunnels; the widest fords; the most beautiful canals; the bendiest bike path; the longest downhills. Weird places where you can (metaphorically) take your bike downhill skiing, potholing or tightrope walking, or turn it into a pedalo. Oddities such as cycling on a motorway or the right-hand side of the road.

We chose them carefully, based on two decades of cycle touring experience. We've spread them round the country, roughly according to population density. Many can be done in a lunchtime; all can be used as an excuse for a day trip or a three-month tour.

All are doable by train, the way we recommend. Of course, you could chuck the bikes in the back of the car, drive up and tick the thing off, and drive back — but this would defeat the point. Because every cycle trip, whether it's down to the shops for a pint of milk or from Land's End to John O'Groats, is a subtle mix of both means and ends. When you set out to do any of the things in this book, be prepared to create memorable experiences not just from the being there but also the getting there. Cycling naturally puts you into the encounters with people, places, and often weather, that make for the satisfying glow afterwards as you relate your stories to friends and family over dinner or a drink. All one-off, unrepeatable things unique to your particular journey, maybe unconnected with the target. But without that target, you wouldn't have had them.

So we hope this book gives you a set of 50 targets that turns into 50, or more, memorable days out where something else might happen entirely. You'll be swopping stories with other cyclists about what happened to you when you set out to cross the country's longest cyclable bridge, penetrate the loneliest tunnel, ride on an original Roman Road, summon a ferry with a table-tennis bat, beat the tide across to Holy Island, or descend the steepest street in England.

Even how you can be the top cyclist in the British Isles. In altitude terms, at least.

Rob Ainsley

eye**Opener**

Why Eye published this book

Every work day I cycle twenty-five miles to and from the office, a hazardous undertaking in London traffic at the best of times, but less so when I am properly tuned into my environment. At Eye Books we take pride in publishing books that we hope do just that: opening the eyes of our readers to the opportunities all around, the environment and communities in which we live – challenging the way we see things.

I had met our author, Rob Ainsley, a number of times before we began working together on this book. Rob and his partner Rebecca are avid cyclists and are actively involved in London cycling. Eye Books has published a number of cycling books (see page 220), providing reason for our paths to cross.

Cultivating the Eye Books community of authors and readers and supporting our local community is one of the pillars upon which Eye Books is built. And each year Eye Books holds a Christmas event when we open our offices to the public and invite them to enjoy mince pies and mulled wine, see what we do, hopefully buy books and join our community. In December 2006 Rob dropped in to pick up some presents for his friends and family and we got talking about a book that he had written. Rob's sense of humour and adventure was also familiar to me through his authorship of a number of the best-selling Bluffer's Guides® so I knew we were on for a fun ride.

I just knew that 50 Quirky Bike Rides ... in England and Wales would be a great addition to the Eye Books list. As well as being community oriented, Eye Books has a campaigning ethos. And in this respect it is to 'Get on your bike!' I was reminded of the saying of Confucius that 'a journey of a thousand miles begins with a single step' and so it is that a cycle ride begins with a single pedal. If we are to encourage others to get on their bikes we must give them reason to do so. Perhaps there is no better reason to do so than for fun. And this is what 50 quirky rides is all about – having fun on your bike, whether you are an advanced cyclist, just a beginner or a family. This book offers great suggestions for people wishing to do this, and wherever you may be based in England or Wales there is something nearby for that exciting day trip or if from further afield a weekend on a bizarre bike ride.

Cycling is something I believe we should all do more of and if this book helps anyone get on their bike then it will be worthwhile. Cycling makes you feel good, get fit and helps reduce carbon footprints. Do it and enjoy.

Dan Hiscocks
Publisher
Dan@Eye-Books.com

Maps for each ride, and other goodies
Visit www.BizarreBiking.com to look up the ride.

AND —

Share your own favourite Quirky Bike Rides;
Visit www.BizarreBiking.com for how to send your stories and
pictures to us.

ROMAN ROAD (of course)

East Whelan

Hiscocks Fm

PH

PH

PH

LC

PH (rems of)

T R

RUTLAND WATER

Joseph Close

riverside café

Great Dun Fell

RTER BRIDGES

Ferry, cross the Mersey,
cause this land's the place I love

cycle path

Philippa Crescent

Victoria Close

Hiscocks Road

Whelan

Robinson Road

Brendan Close

Rebecca Avenue

riverside bars
and restaurants

bridge

beach

London City Airport

Docklands

O2 Dome

Greenwich tunnel

Thames Barrier

start/end at
train station

riverside pubs

Woolwich Ferry

1 Hill Locks

www.BizarreBiking.com

Contents

Contents

BIZARRE BIKING

29 quirky symbols
used throughout this book

Steep

Wet

Ferry ride

Canal

Bridges

Tunnel

Train

Roman road

Extreme

Weird

Smooth

Bumpy

Really bumpy

Snacks

Drinks

Family ride

Straightforward

Tricky

Complicated

Time
dependent

Pricey

Exciting

Knackering

Cars

50 quirky rides

all over England and Wales

GOLD HILL

WHERE *Dorset: Gillingham-Shaftesbury, 10km one way*

WHAT *England's most famous cycling hill*

WHY *Re-enact the Hovis advert on your bike*

HOW *Train to Gillingham*

This is a **10km ride from the station in Gillingham** to the hill town of Shaftesbury, along quiet country back roads. There's not a great deal to see en route, but your destination Shaftesbury has Hardyesque charm, cafes and pubs – and England's most famous TV cycling moment for you to re-enact: the 1970s Hovis advert, which was set on the town's Gold Hill.

Rattle down England's best-known cycling hill

From Gillingham station, head north-east towards East Knoyle, then south towards Motcombe along the signposted North Dorset Cycleway. From there it's a couple of kilometres climb up to Shaftesbury. (The B3081 south-east is shorter but it's a busy and narrow road.)

In Shaftesbury, keep going up to the main street, reassuringly equipped with cottagey pubs named

brated commercial. It was first screened in 1973, and was supposedly voted the best ever UK television commercial of all time. The ad was repeated briefly in May 2006 as part of a retrospective campaign.

The film, entitled *Bike Round*, sees a baker's delivery boy pushing his bike up the cobbled street of some pre-Great-War village for his final call of the day. He clatters his

after ceremonial headgear. Gold Hill runs south from here. You'll see it signposted, a narrow cobbled pedestrian alley running down to the right of the town hall. A few metres down, it opens out into a small cobbled square. There's a cafe, where you can sit outside and watch tourists not quite knowing what to do next, and a rather unappetising Hovis-loaf monument the size of an office desk. Gold Hill curves its stony, traffic-free, way down to the right, bordered by the old Abbey walls on the right, and thatched cottages on the left.

Walk your bike down the footpath, and turn round to re-enact the cele-

way back down to the baker's, and is rewarded with slabs of Hovis. Accompanying it is a brass-band arrangement of the Largo from Dvorak's *New World Symphony*, and a voiceover, clearly of the boy, who is now an old man.

Many people assume the ad was set in Yorkshire, partly because of the brass band, partly because of a subsequent lampoon in a novelty single by South Yorkshire comedian Andy Capstick. (His spoof was in 1981, which shows how enduring the original was.) But the narrator's accent in the film is definitely West Country, not West Riding. The boy actor showed a fair bit of skill in staying upright while shuddering down the cobbles on that ancient rod-brake machine.

Here are the original words: "Last stop on t' round would be old Ma Peggotty's place," as you push up you reminisce about an epoch so distant definite articles had not fully evolved. "'Twas like taking bread to the top of the world!" Turn round and rattle downhill. "'Twas a grand ride back though," you continue, twasly. The tourists sitting outside the cafe at the top of the hill will be taking pictures of you. And pointing at you. And sniggering.

To re-enact the rest of the ad you can visit one of the bakeries in the centre of town, or one of the pubs: "And aaafterward, I knew baker would 'ave kettle on and doorsteps of 'ot 'Ovis ready. 'There's 'olemeal in 'Ovis,' he'd say. 'Get it inside you, lad. Does you good, that. One day you'll go up that hill as faaast as you come dewn!'" Finish with the 1973-style Voice of Authority, obviously a chap with a pipe. "Hoe-vis," you say, mindful of your elocution lessons. "It's ez good for yew todayyy, ez it's warlways beeyan".

It's much harder than it looks, but it is every bit as scenic

Forum. National Cycle Route 25 (Longleat to Poole) also links Gillingham with Shaftesbury.

Gillingham – hard g, like a fish's gill – was the subject of five paintings by Constable, and there's a small museum about them. It's hard to see what he'd find to paint these days. About 8km north of Gillingham is Stourhead, a National Trust stately home with absurdly picturesque grounds and gardens. Blandford Forum, which was entirely rebuilt after a fire in 1731, is famous as a consistent and well-preserved Georgian market town. It's about 20km south of Shaftesbury.

Gold Hill itself is a part of a 6000km long leisure cycleway round Britain's back lanes called the National Byway system,

■ Also in the area

The North Dorset Cycleway (Regional Route 41) is a picturesque signed circular route of 120km or so linking Gillingham with Shaftesbury and Blandford

www.thenationalbyway.org. It was, coincidentally, first sponsored by Hovis, hence the wheatsheaf logo on the signs.

At the top of Gold Hill, you can turn left through a little alley and cycle by a small hilltop park with sweeping views over the Dorset prairies. A good place for a picnic, if you don't fancy the local cafes.

From Shaftesbury you're not that far from the Bath, Bristol and Devizes-based items in this book – *see pages 18-25.*

■ Other places like this

If you can't get to Shaftesbury, there are other steep, cobbled, cottagey streets in English towns where you can reenact the advert.

Some likely candidates might be Steep Hill, Lincoln; Mermaid St in Rye, Sussex *(pictured, left)*; Keere St in Lewes, Sussex; Catherine Hill in Frome, Somerset; the main street of Haworth, Yorkshire; Waterbag Bank, Knaresborough, Yorkshire; the main street of Robin Hood's Bay, Yorkshire *(see page 162)*; and Front St and Market Place, Alston, Cumbria *(see page 164).*

The much-photographed main street of Clovelly in Devon is famously so steep that it is a series of cobbled steps, barred to traffic and plied only by pedestrians, hand-drawn sledges, and tourists wielding digital cameras. You could presumably clump your way down on a bike with locomotive-grade shock absorbers but we don't know anyone who has. Perhaps someone could do it with a pannier of fresh cream and see if it is whipped by the time you get to the bottom.

If you're stuck in gradient-poor, cottage-free London, you'll need your imagination to re-enact the Hovis experience. Try a posh cobbled mews, perhaps in northish westish London around Hyde Park, turn your camera at an angle, then lie about it afterwards.

Snackstop

The Salt Cellar, Gold Hill. *Classy cafe right at the top of the hill, with fine views down the cobbled street and to the vale beyond.*

Bevvy break

Ship Inn, High Street. *14th-century traditional pub with real ale, 100m or so beyond top of Gold Hill, substantially inland but mystifyingly decked out with maritime apparel.*

Quirkshop

Blandford Forum's rebuilding was supervised by brothers William and John Bastard from 1731-60. So you can point to any of the market square's fine Georgian facades and say, "Which Bastard designed that?", and you're actually asking a very intelligent question.

Tourer's tick list

✓ Picnic panorama in park by Gold Hill
✓ Stourhead gardens
✓ Blandford Forum

OS 183, grid ref ST861228
INFO Shaftesbury & Gillingham Tourist Information Service, 8 Bell St, Shaftesbury, Dorset SP7 8AE,
tel. 01747 853514,
tourism@shaftesburydorset.com

BATH BRADFORD AQUEDUCTS

WHERE *Somerset: Bath-Bradford, 12km one way*

WHAT *England's most picturesque canal path*

WHY *Cycle on two amazing aqueducts, canalside in mid-air*

HOW *Train to Bath or Bradford*

A stretch of flat, traffic-free, lovely scenery on a canal towpath here, from the centre of Bath to the gem of Bradford-on-Avon. *En-route* you have the odd sensation of cycling alongside water, over water: at Dundas and Avoncliff, the Kennet and Avon Canal soars over the River Avon on splendid aqueducts built by John Rennie more than 200 years ago.

Fly over water on Britain's most gorgeous canal path

Coming from Bath (and trying not to be detained too long at the picturebook George pub at Bathampton), you cycle along a few kilometres of towpath that follows a contour halfway up one side of a valley, past clusters of colourful moored narrowboats. Dundas Aqueduct gently ambushes you from behind some trees, turning left in an abrupt right-angle over the Avon. To carry on along the towpath you need to cross over the little humpty-backed bridge. This is engineering poetry that knits together river and canal in a giant aquatic chiasmus; it's quite impressive too.

Just over the tiny drawbridge on the right is an offshoot with an air of the secret passageway about it: the Somerset Coal Canal. A short distance of this has been restored, and this really is for narrow narrowboats. You can cycle down the SCC's towpath a few hundred metres to Brass Knocker Basin. Here there's a good cafe, shop, cycle and canoe hire. Back on the K&A towpath, you can now go across the southern side of the aqueduct.

Dundas Aqueduct is often said to be the finest on Britain's waterways. To appreciate just how elegantly John Rennie and his chums integrated a large piece of civil engineering into the landscape, in much the same way that architects today don't, walk down the steps immediately beyond the aqueduct to the river bank. From here is your best view of the aqueduct's supporting structure.

After an abrupt turn right beyond the aqueduct, there's a few kilometres of straight shady ambling with the river valley down on your right. Just past a little bridge you'll pass a handwritten sign for Fordside Tea Gardens, where you can enjoy home-made tea and cakes in someone's garden. Shortly after you'll come upon the second aqueduct, jagging suddenly to the right back

over the Avon.

This is the village of Avoncliff, which manages to have a railway station, beautiful pub, river, canal and cafe, and about two houses. The labyrinthine lanes that lead to it have always been signposted so obscurely that you wonder if they're trying to keep it secret from car drivers. Let's hope so.

On the aqueduct you can look back up the Avon valley. And the towpath does some topological gymnastics here: you cross over to the left-hand side of the canal by turning right just beyond the aqueduct and crossing underneath the canal. That gets you up and back onto the towpath that continues to

Bradford. But on your way up from under the aqueduct, you go right past the forecourt of a pub and a shop. If your cycling efforts have rendered you in urgent need of (a) aromatherapy, healing crystals and scented candles, or (b) beer and food, then this is the place to stop.

Along the canal you may well see kingfishers (usually glimpsed as a shiny turquoise blur flitting away from you up the waterway) and herons (who stand warily statuesque at the waterside waiting for a fish, then flee laboriously with it).

After exploring Bradford, which is well worth a visit in its own right, you can take the train back to Bath – or else retrace your steps.

Enjoy homemade cakes in a private garden

■ Also in the area

Bath is one of England's hilliest towns, so the level canal route into it is very welcome, as well as fascinating cycling. It takes you into the town along the side, past one of the deepest locks in the country, and in what you might call the back entrance, by the railway station to the south. Once at the station, you can head north for all the day-tripper stuff. West is the Bath–Bristol Railway Path, the UK's best rail trail *(see Staple Hill, page 22)*. The canal path is all part of Sustrans'

National Cycle Route 4, which goes from London to St David's on the Welsh coast.

There's a very good website guide to the canal paths round Bath and Bradford, which you can find at www.paulspages.co.uk. Georgian Bath, simperingly touristy as it may be with teddy bear shops, platinum-card restaurants and Edinburgh Woollen Mill, is still a place that you have to visit. After a six-year delay, the hot spa is now open to the public, though you're unlikely to get in without a reservation. If it's a hot day and you fancy a swim, do what the locals do and skinny-dip in the river at Warleigh Weir. You'll have to ask directions from a local, but it's good fun trying.

Llangollen *(see page 130)*. The canal over the North Circular in London is pretty startling too *(see page 66)*. For more nice towpath cycling routes, a browse of Sustrans' website or handbook will suggest some other possibilities all around the country. For scenic effect the Monmouth and Brecon Canal comes to mind: 50km of National Park splendour between Brecon and Pontypool, although a few sections are not practical for cycling. Check the website at www.waterscape.com. The 200km Leeds & Liverpool Canal is one of three canals that crosses the Pennines, and has some thrilling scenery. All the Yorkshire section is open to cyclists *(see page 30; though rural parts beyond the excellent Bingley-Leeds stretch can be grassy and muddy)*.

■ Other places like this

A precarious and scarier counterpart to the sturdy poise of Rennie's aqueduct is at Pontcysyllte near

---

Snackstop
Brass Knocker Basin, Dundas Aqueduct. *Picturesque, good quality visitor-centre cafe; sit outside in the sun.*

Bevvy break
Cross Guns, Avoncliff. *Front garden tumbles down to the Constable-like riverbank, good real ale, regal puddings.*

Quirkshop
Despite the one-way system, hillls and tourist road-crossers looking the wrong way, Bath and its golden Georgian architecture is fine for exploring by bike. Cycle across photogenic Pulteney Bridge, which crosses the Avon a kilometre north from the station. It's one of only four bridges in the world with shops all along both sides, and one of not enough bridges in the world prohibited to cars.

Tourer's tick list
✓ Explore Georgian Bath by bike
✓ Cycle Pulteney Bridge
✓ Coal canal spur
✓ Riverside Bradford
✓ Picnic by river
✓ Herons, kingfishers

OS (1) 172, grid ref ST785625
(2) 173, grid ref ST805600
INFO www.paulspages.co.uk

STAPLE HILL TUNNEL

WHERE *Bath to Bristol, 22km*

WHAT *Smooth, scenic, traffic-free rail trail*

WHY *England's best rail trail, and best cycling tunnel*

HOW *Train to Bristol or Bath*

The Bristol and Bath Railway Path is England's best cycle route: easy day-trip length, level, skatable-smooth, scenic, and car-free. Linking two cities, with train access at both ends, and with plenty to see en route, there are artworks, sculptures, drinking fountains, restored bridges, fabulous river views, a steam railway, and numerous pubs on or just off the way. It also has the best cycle-tunnel experience you'll get.

The perfect cycling day ride, and a brilliant bike tunnel

Bristol to Bath is the best direction to enjoy the 22km path. The start is signposted, only 2km from Bristol Temple Meads station. The first few kilometres of the B&BRP are urban and bustling. You go through the greenish but inner-city area of Fishponds (notable for a big brick fish), past a supermarket, and about 7km from the start you find Staple Hill Tunnel, 471m of cylindrical, sodium-lit delight.

In the couple of minutes it takes to cycle through you'll begin to understand what all those ferrets see in scurrying up and down long tubes. Unlike the sonic bedlam of road tunnels, roiling with trapped engine noise and fumes, Staple Hill Tunnel is fresh, cool, and quiet. Well, quiet until a cyclist whooshes through impersonating coloratura-soprano dogs, cackling demons or full-throttle steam locomotives. There's a little drippy condensation in the tunnel's deepest recesses, but you're unlikely to need a towel. It's long enough to be exciting, not long enough to be tedious, and the light at the end of the tunnel really is light, and not a hoodie with a torch.

Shortly after the tunnel is the old Mangotsfield station, where another line used to branch off to Gloucester, which is good to explore by bike. Sculptures congregate here, including some giant pencils. At Warmley's old station, about 10km from the start, there are silhouette sculptures on the platform, occasional cafes, and the only public toi-

let on the track. Nearing Bitton is a drinking fountain in the shape of a flat-nosed Roman Arthur Mullard, and a restored railway line, which you cross to reach Bitton station.

The 8km from here to Bath is the loveliest stretch on the trail, and it crosses the River Avon several times, passing by picturesque riverside pubs. The only pub directly on the cycle path is the Bird in Hand in Saltford, which you'll see as you are crossing the Avon, a few kilometres out of Bath. The Bird in Hand is a fine choice, but even more atmospheric is the Jolly Sailor a kilometre

■ Also in the area

For more civil engineering thrills in Bristol, ride over the Clifton Suspension Bridge, 4km west from Temple Meads station and along the river *(see page 18)*. Or try in vain to cycle up Britain's steepest street *(see page 14)*. From the city centre you can cycle alongside the south side of the Avon, which takes you under Clifton's bridge.

The B&BRP takes you directly to Bath railway station. Bath's fun to roam by bike, but the Rubik-cube one-way streets and steep hills mean you'll spend quite a bit of time walking. The best area to explore is either side of the river up to Pulteney Bridge, with its hyperbolic weir, and the grand Georgian terraces round about it. The cobbled tourist draw of Royal Crescent is a kilometre or so north-west from here, in Victoria Park, a fine place for a cycling picnic on a sunny day.

The Kennet and Avon canal comes off the River Avon just by Bath railway station, and you can cycle along its towpath. You go past some excitingly deep locks, under bridges and past a park, and enjoy some splendid sideways views of the town. The towpath continues east in beautiful scenery and involves two fabulous aqueducts – *see page 18*.

away. Come off at the Bird in Hand and head along the lane on the opposite side, along the river. The Jolly Sailor has food and real ale, and is right on a weir with lovely views from the gardens, right at the waterside. You arrive in the outskirts of Bath at an industrial estate, and continue along the towpath of the Avon right into the city centre. Here you can hop on a train, or cycle farther along the canal *(see page 18 for this, and for more about Bath)*. If you keep following the path of the canal, you'll get to the Thames and so eventually to London, all on the flat. Well, almost flat. More information on the canal paths around this area can be found on an excellent website at www.paulspages.co.uk.

> *You'll understand what all those ferrets like about long tubes*

■ Other places like this

If long, traffic-free tunnels is what you're talking about, on a rail trail, there's a similar experience on the West Country Way. This is another Sustrans route that goes from Cornwall to Somerset taking in such routes as the Camel Trail from Padstow *(see page 26)* and the Tarka Trail between Braunton and Meeth – one of the longest traffic-free cycle paths in the country. On the Tarka, just south of Bideford, you go through a long lit tunnel very similar to Staple Hill, except that it's gently curved, making it more like a Swiss physics lab's particle accelerator than ferret's practice drainpipe *(pictured right)*.

More tunnels may be on the way, and in the Bath area too. There's currently a plan (for details see www.twotunnels.org.uk) to develop a disused railway running south of Bath into a 7km-long railtrail. This would involve restoring two tunnels under the hills of the town's housing-covered southern slopes: the 409m Devonshire Tunnel, and just to the south of it, the 807m Combe Down Tunnel. If and when completed that would be the longest rail-trail tunnel in the UK, and the longest traffic-free tunnel explicitly open to cyclists.

Snackstop

The Buffet, Bitton Station. *Splendid home-made cakes ideal for cyclists with a cup of tea, right on the cycle path.*

Bevvy break

The Jolly Sailor, Saltford. *Riverside beer gardens, fine beer and food, wonderful scenery – lock your bike well!*

Quirkshop

Britain's deepest canal lock is in Bath centre. It's on the canal that branches off the River Avon just east of the railway station. Cycle a few metres east along the canal towpath and you'll see the awesome locks in front of you. When the canal was restored in 1976, Locks 8 and 9 were combined to make one with a descent of nearly 6m, the country's sheerest drop.

Tourer's tick list

✓ Explore Bath
✓ Bristol dockside
✓ Clifton Suspension Bridge
✓ Avon Valley Railway
✓ Sculpture-spot along route, and Mangotsfield spur

OS 172, grid ref ST651757
INFO Bristol Tourist Information,Travel Centre, 11 Colston Av, Bristol BS1 4UB, ticharbourside @ destinationbristol.co.uk; www.paulspages.co.uk

The Eden Project

CLAY TRAILS

WHERE *Between Par and St Austell, Cornwall*

WHAT *Three short traffic free paths converging on Eden Project, 5km-8km each*

WHY *Weird scenery, and discounts for cyclists at Eden Project*

HOW *Train to Par, St Austell, or Bugle*

This is a selection of three family-friendly, traffic-free paths that offer weird scenery, and the rewarding experience of being paid to cycle – kind of. Because if you visit the Eden Project by bike, you receive fast-track entry and a big discount. If you've ever had the experience of a snooty restaurant, office or hotel looking down their nose at you because you arrived by bike, this will balance things out.

Be rewarded for cycling amid strange, spectacular scenery

The three Clay Trail bike routes are the Bugle (6.5km), Wheal Martyn (8km), and Par Beach (5km) trails. Like innocence itself, they all end at Eden. They're short – even very young, very old, or very scared riders will be able to cope – but they're delightful and traffic-free. An excellent downloadable guide, complete with maps and details is available on Sustrans' own very good website, www.sustrans.org. uk – search for Clay Trails.

The trails each start at, or go through, railway stations: at Bugle, St Austell and Par respectively. The easiest access for the cyclist coming in by train is to go west from the railway station at Par, on the route between Par Beach (which is only a couple of hundred metres south of the station) and St Blazey (which is a couple of kilometres from Eden along quiet but hilly Cornhill Lane).

It's a spectacular and often strange landscape round here, with massive white spoil heaps from the clay pits and turquoise inland lakes. The huge snowy cone behind St Austell looks jarringly out of place, as if a nostalgic Hokusai had drawn a cartoon Mount Fuji to make a postcard home.

The great geodesic domes of the Eden Project house gardens and greenhouses which replicate the climates and plant life of many regions of the world. Built in an old quarry, it is quite fascinating. Everyone we know who's been has loved it, especially our mums. Arrive by bike and you get three quid discount, and

fast-track entry. There are covered bike racks, close to the entrance, and lockers too. Entry is normally £13.80, with concessions down to £7; opening hours are 10am-4.30pm winter, 9am-6pm summer. The cycle route in is scenic – far more so than the vehicle route, which is meticulously landmarked by branches of Tesco and McDonald's on Eden's website map.

Your final approach on bikes to the Project is through a wood, with the Project's weird scifi buildings suddenly appearing below in the site of an old clay pit. The golfball-shaped hothouses, the 'biomes',

look like they might house top-secret radar installations or NASA prototypes of a Mars colony, rather than perspiring giant salads.

An easy day trip might consist of going from Par to the Project along the Par Beach trail, and from the Project to St Austell along the Wheal

Martyn Trail, from where you could catch a train for home. The Wheal Martyn Trail offers you the biggest scenery of the three, and at one point includes a panorama that takes in the whole bay of St Austell to the south and the bizarre remnants of the clay industry spread out to the north, east and west. A fourth Clay Trail is on the way, and said to be coming soon.

> *...as if Hokusai had drawn a cartoon Mount Fuji for a postcard home*

■ Also in the area

If you only want to get to the Eden Project and aren't bothered about the trails, you can cycle east to it along roads from St Austell station, though there's not much point.

If you're up for a few day's cycle tour, Sustrans National Cycle Route 3 (which links Bristol and Land's End) carries on west from St Austell to Mevagissey. If you fancy something less horizontal, Cornwall's coast is an astonishingly beautiful ride. It can be a bit tough and rugged for touring, though. If you don't mind hills you might want to cycle down to The Lizard, Britain's most southerly point, and round to Land's End, the island's traditional 'end point' *(see page 210 for Land's End to John O'Groats)*. If you're collecting other extreme points, the easternmost is at Lowestoft in Suffolk, the westernmost at Ardnamurchan Point just north of Mull in Scotland, and the northernmost at Dunnet Head, next door to the other end point

John O'Groats.

The Eden Project is too far away from the Camel Trail *(see page 26)* for all but dedicated tourers.

Eden's bike-friendliness is complemented by plenty of cycle-hire and guided-cycle-tour opportunities: Happy Trails in Bugle (01726 852058) offers accompanied rides to Eden on your own bike from Pentewan, Bugle and Carlyon Bay (adults £15). Bike hire is available from Pentewan Valley in Pentewan (01726 844242), Bugle Cycle Hire in Bugle (01726 852285), and also from Barlow's in St Austell (01726 73117).

■ Other places like this

There are a number of other places which offer discount to those who arrive by bike, though none as lavishly encouraging as the Eden Project. One place keen to offer a bounty to cyclists is the Centre for Alternative Technology, 5km north of Machynlleth railway station in mid-north-Wales. It costs you £5 instead of £6 to get in and see their very interesting eco-stuff exhibits – wind turbines, smart compost heaps, special gardens, and a cyclegenerator so you can see just how much work is involved in keeping a light bulb going (lots, incidentally, which makes you realise how much electricity must be used by those pesky outdoor heaters they put in pub beer gardens these days).

A few dozen National Trust properties also offer special rates for bikes, such as Lydford Gorge *(pictured right)*. Usually what you'll get is a quid discount, though a couple of places also offer some vouchers or a free cup of tea. The National Trust website has a full list at www.nationaltrust.org.

During National Bike Week (in the middle of June; see www.bikeweek. org.uk) some places also offer one-off freebies or discounts to those turning up on bicycles. Details are available at the website or in the local press. Some London attractions are decent for cycle parking and general attitude to bikes (Tate Modern, London Aquarium, Kew Gardens, National Theatre) and some bad (Madam Tussaud's, St Paul's Cathedral, London Zoo, London Eye).

Snackstop

Jo's Cafe, Eden Project. *Several fine cafes in the Project put emphasis on local food. Jo's does good coffee too.*

Bevvy break

Seven Stars Inn, East Hill. *In St Austell town centre in front of the train station is this friendly locals' place. Serves the local St Austell beer.*

Quirkshop

St Austell wouldn't be top of too many people's must-see lists, but there are some good beaches. Porthpean is less than 5km south-east and quite popular; Polkerris, further east past Carlyon, is quieter. St Austell's picturesque old port, Charlestown, was the setting for the BBC costume drama 'Poldark'.

Tourer's tick list

✓ Beaches
✓ Views of 'Mount Fuji'

OS 200, grid ref SX050551
INFO St Austell Tourist Information Centre, Southbourne Road, St Austell, Cornwall PL25 4RS, tel. 01726 879500, tic@cornish-riviera.co.uk; www.edenproject.com

Caen Hill Locks

CAEN HILL

WHERE *Bradford on Avon, Somerset, to Devizes, Wiltshire, 16km one way*

WHAT *Traffic-free canal towpath*

WHY *Astonishing flight of 16 locks; the UK's longest downhill towpath*

HOW *Train to Bradford on Avon*

Flat, traffic-free, and with characterful towns at either end, this is a fantastic half-day canal towpath for all cycling abilities (or day trip, if you do it return). It's part of Sustrans' National Cycle Route 4, and part of its Thames and Severn Valley Route. And it offers you one of the most extraordinary sights on the waterways – Caen Hill's aquatic escalator of 16 locks in a dead straight line – and the long cycle downhill, on a canal.

Cycle downhill along a waterway wonder

Start from the train station at Bradford. It's a charming honey-stone small town, a kind of pet Bath. The back lanes and riverside areas are worth exploring, perhaps for a picnic. Head a kilometre south to the canal. From here you head east along the towpath about 16km towards Devizes. It's mostly 'sooth-ing' (ie not breathtaking, but pleas-antly English) inter-town canal scenery: a marina, a few narrow-boats with smiley middle-aged cou-ples waving at you, one or two quaint bridges with historic pubs, and flat open fields either side. But just outside Devizes, after you pass under a small road bridge, comes

up to Devizes and double back on road.)

It's an easy ascent – and of course you have a fabulous downhill in the bank for your return trip back. Chat to the narrowboaters slogging their way through the gates. They'll cer-tainly have the time: it takes three hours to do this stretch on a good day, and on a bad day, a day. And in all there are 29 locks in a 4km stretch here, raising the canal 72m. They were the last part of the canal – a vital water transport link between Bristol and London – to be completed in 1810.

A friendly cafe sits at the top, with a view not quite as dramatic as you

your reward, and it's really some-thing: Caen Hill's 16 locks shoot up before you in a dead straight line, as if the canal was taking off.

This isn't the longest sequence of locks in the country; Tardebigge in Worcestershire has 30. But Caen Hill's is the most photographable. (The best place to snap it is from that little humpback bridge you've just cycled under, which is on the B3101 to Rowde – irritatingly, there's no quick way from the bridge on to the towpath. You have to go

might hope. From here it's another couple of kilometres into Devizes itself. At the wharf in the town cen-tre, there's a Canal Visitor Centre, canal museum and shop (with free cycling guides to the area). There are plenty of pubs in the town, and a malty aroma heralds Wadworths, the brewery responsible for 6X, which is clearly fifty per cent better than Australian lager.

A sobering thought for your lunchtime pint is that we very near-ly lost this canal. Britain's water-

ways fell into neglect through the 20th century and by the 1970s, like many other parts of the network, Caen Hill was derelict. Thanks to restoration work, much of it by volunteers, the lock system was good as new by 1990, completing the final link in the revival of the Kennet & Avon Canal.

■ Also in the area

The 40km canal route west, back to Bath, is one of the most beautiful easy-cycling routes in the UK. National Cycle Route 4, which runs from London west, through Reading, Bath and Bristol to St David's in west Wales, runs a few kilometres north of Devizes. See the Bath-Bradford Aqueducts feature *(page 18)*.

Devizes is also on a southern alternative section of the Sustrans Severn &

Thames Cycle Route, running 200km from Newbury to Gloucester. You can carry on east along the Kennet & Avon beyond Devizes almost all the way to Reading. Little Honeystreet, eight kilometres or so past Devizes, has a characterful old canal pub where you can camp.

This area of England is known for its dozen or so white horses cut into the chalky hillsides. Devizes has two, an old and new one (see Quirkshop) and most of the others are within cycling distance, in off-the-beaten sort of places. Collect the set over a long weekend for a cycling trip with a twist. Apart from Devizes, there are horses at Alton Barnes; Broad Town; Cherhill; Broad Hinton; Marlborough; Pewsey; and the most dramatic at Westbury (see www.wiltshirewhitehorses. org.uk).

A few miles north of Alton Barnes is Avebury, whose ancient stone circle is like Stonehenge, except that it's a pleasure to visit and isn't full of damn tourists. Its cosy village (pub and all) is situated within the ring of smaller but

> *An aquatic escalator of 16 locks in a dead straight line*

friendlier stones, which you can not only cycle round and through, but also clamber on if you feel so inclined. And it's free. If you're up for a long hilltop offroad excursion, the Ridgeway starts here.

Other places like this

A large list of lock flights, though not all will be cyclable, is at www.jim-shead.com/waterways /LockFlights.html.

One of our favourite stretches of downhill canal towpath is at Hanwell in West London, on the Grand Union a couple of miles north-west of Brentford *(pictured left, on page 31)*: a smooth and beautiful coast down from Southall's multicultural curries to Brentford's Singapore-shiny office blocks. You can slice right through north London on canals from here: all the way from here via Paddington, Regents Park, Kings Cross, Islington, along some more

locks and hairy descents under narrow bridges on Regents Canal, and right up to Stratford in north-west London, home of the 2012 Olympics *(See page 66)*.

A lock sequence which is as celebrated as Caen Hill, but very different, is Bingley's Five Rise Locks *(pictured left, on page 32)*. Astoundingly steep and abrupt, the five staircase locks (in other words, the top gate of one is the bottom of the next) are a dramatic episode in a delightful day's cycling along the scenic Leeds & Liverpool Canal. Start at Leeds, and ride at leisure to time-capsule Saltaire, a World Heritage site built as a model village for Victorian factory workers and virtually unchanged today. Make the Five Rise ascent, and then either cycle or take the train back to Leeds.

Snackstop
Caen Hill Locks Cafe. *Lovely and friendly little place; sit outside with your bike and with a view.*

Bevvy break
Bridge Inn, Horton. *Three kilometres along the canal path beyond Devizes: canalside pub with garden and 6X.*

Quirkshop
Devizes has two hillside white horses: an old one, now invisible, on the edge of Roundway Down; and a new one, cut in 1999. Take the canal path about a kilometre past Devizes town centre, and turn left at the bridge (crossing the A361) to take the lane to Roundway village. It's visible from here, and there's a footpath that leads right up to the horse itself.

Tourer's tick list
✓ Explore Bradford
✓ Devizes wharf
✓ White horses
✓ Avebury

OS 173, grid ref ST977615
INFO Canal Visitor Centre, Devizes Wharf,
tel. 01380 721279, www.katrust.org

BOSHAM HARBOUR

WHERE   *West Sussex: Bosham to Chichester, 12km one way*

WHAT   *Quiet back lanes from a unique harbour to historic Chichester*

WHY   *Your bike is a canoe: cycle on the surface of the sea*

HOW   *Train to Bosham*

This is an easy roll along a Sustrans path through gentle coast-flat scenery, finishing with Roman villas and historic cathedrals – and starting with the remarkable feat of cycling on the seawater. If you time it right, anyway.

Cycle on water!
Turn your bike into a pedalo

The trim harbourside village of Bosham, near Chichester on the south coast, lets you cycle on water most days. It's all thanks to the horseshoe-shaped waterfront and Shore Road, whose surface is about 4.5m or so above sea level. High tide levels through the year vary between 3m and 5m, so the tarmac is frequently covered, even submerged. Start your trip here; the village centre is a couple of km south of the railway station, and signposted.

For the best water-skimming experience, come when the high tide is about 4.5m or a bit higher.

float away because the water seeps inside, except perhaps those famously watertight Beetles. A VW owner might like to test this theory, and send us pictures of the results.)

Highest tides occur just after equinox full moons. Various websites predict high-tide times and levels. It was in Bosham, sometime around the 1020s, that Canute supposedly issued his command for the tide to turn back.

A bike is the ideal way to experience Bosham's regular maritime inundations. Not only can you do your two-wheeled duck impression, you can also flit between the vari-

Then you'll get an hour or so of high tide with the road surface just covered, just enough to turn your bike into a two-wheeled pedalo.

For the most spectacular experience, come when there's a really high tide of 5m or more. You'll see the water's edge move up closer and closer to the front doors of harbourside houses; tourists with inappropriate footwear trying to get across flooded lanes; and maybe the odd vehicle left by an inattentive owner being gently immersed. (Cars don't

ous theatres of aquatic development. When the harbour road gets flooded, there's a lane behind the pub that also links the waterside shop, cafe and parking area, with the harbour and the back of the pub, so you can zip between the bits of action.

If you are intent on some splashing activity, bring sandals and a towel. On a bright day the shallow waters, warmed by sunshine and grilled tarmac, are delightfully warm to wade through. But salt water does terrible things to chains and drive trains, so do rinse and lube them afterwards, unless you enjoy the sound of pepper grinders.

Do your two-wheeled duck impression

At low tide, you can cycle across the bridle path that runs across the middle of the harbour. It gives neat views of the waterfront, and if you come on a low high-tide day, you can still get something of the water-skimming experience here, as it's quite a bit lower than the road level, and so it floods here first. It's a bit gravelly though, and if you go off-piste you will sink into the mud, so watch out.

Watching a car succumb slowly to the tide is a sobering reminder of man's hubris confounded by Nature's might. It's also a really good laugh at someone else's expense. When the water reaches

case, it ends up a write-off. People's reactions demonstrate the Four Personality Types: *Type 1* "Oh dear, how terrible for the owner". *Type 2* "Hah! Serves 'em right for not reading the signs!" *Type 3* "Omigod! Is ours alright?" *Type 4* "That's a Y-reg Vectra! It's an insurance scam!"

From Bosham, head anti-clockwise round the coast to Fishbourne and ultimately Chichester (which has a train station, of course) along the Sustrans back-lanes cycle routes.

◼ Also in the area

There's some pleasant cycling round the Chichester harbour area for a day trip or more. (The whole harbour is designated as an Area of Outstanding Natural Beauty, though

the electrics the unfortunate vehicle starts to convulse: the central locking clunks on and off, windows run manically up and down, the hazard warning lights flash. Maybe even the car alarm burbles hopefully and the airbags inflate in vain as if to float the thing to safety. In any

it's best appreciated from a boat.) The route that takes you from Bosham to Fishbourne is Sustrans National Cycle Route 2 (Dover to St Austell). Fishbourne is home of some of Britain's best Roman mosaics. The most famous of the twenty or so is the stunning Boy on a Dolphin, no doubt the only way he could get home after his chariot was parked carelessly close to the water's edge. At Fishbourne you switch to the Centurion Way, another Sustrans route. That takes you in another couple of miles (partly along a canal) to Chichester, cathedral and all.

You can cycle out south of Chichester along the Chichester Canal towpath for a few kilometres, and explore the coastal towns and villages such as East Wittering and Selsey Bill.

Just south of Bosham, a kilometre beyond the south-harbour road, is a seasonal passenger ferry to West Itchenor, a harbourside village with a pub.

Other places like this

Bosham is in many ways the most pleasant non-crossing-tidal-road experience for cyclists, but there are many others. You can see a comprehensive list of them at the excellent www.wetroads.co.uk website, in its 'tidal roads' section.

Indeed, there's a similar but more modest example at nearby Sidlesham, half an hour's cycle from Bosham, at the reedy edge of Pagham Harbour. Others include Askham in Cumbria; Aveton Gifford in Devon; Alverstoke in Hampshire; Oulton Boad in Suffolk.

The Thames Path, at very high tides, routinely floods in short stretches at places such as Putney, Richmond, and East Molesey (where you'll see vehicles parked precariously on the sloping concrete riverside by the boathouses). If you do come to a wet bit, there are always civilised ways round just alongside, though.

The fabled crossing to Lindisfarne is England's grandest tidal road *(see page 190).*

Snackstop

Old Bosham Tea Room, Bosham Walk Craft Centre. *Usual cake/coffee/cream tea opportunities at harbourfront; if locking bike outside ensure it's high up.*

Bevvy break

Anchor Bleu, Bosham. *Yes, 'bleu': good pub with all tidal info, decent range of cask ales, and delightful little harbourside terrace where you can have lunch as you watch the tide come in and the cars go under.*

Quirkshop

Bosham's early 11th-century church is pictured on the Bayeux Tapestry. It shows Harold going to the church, then telling William of Normandy he was claiming the Throne of England. The Battle of Hastings ensued.

Tourer's tick list

✓ Cross-harbour bridleway
✓ Quiet waterside villages
✓ Roman mosaics at Fishbourne
✓ Chichester cathedral
✓ West Wittering beach (only if hot)

OS 197, grid ref SU805038
INFO www.bbc.co.uk/weather/coast/tides

Crossing the Channel in style
from Dover to Calais
by luxury ferry

DOVER TO CALAIS

WHERE *Anywhere from Calais, France, to Singapore (2km-20,000km)*

WHAT *Day trip via ferry to abroad*

WHY *Glorious feeling of rolling off the ferry on your bike*

HOW *Combined train-ferry ticket London-Calais*

Rolling off a ferry into another country is something special. Part of the thrill is that you may well be first off: you are waved off down the vibromassage ramp by swarms of wasp-men in grimy amber oilskins, while lines of booze cruisers and bleary-eyed HGV drivers have to wait for you. You briefly have the cement savannah to yourself as you look for a trail out that won't be stampeded by herds of migrating lorries.

Cycle off the ferry to Africa, Asia... or a Calais bistro

Customs and passport control wave you through and out as if you were next door's cat that had wandered into their living room. The juggernaut fleets of Willi Betz, Norbert Dentressangle and Eddie Stobart thunder away into oblivion on an autoroute; you leave the ferry area by a quiet back road, and you have the Continent to yourself. And suddenly a thought strikes you: you are

return (twice that for Paris). The tickets are not well publicised though – you'll find little about it on the Internet (apart from on the excellent, reliable railway travel website www.seat61.com). Buying them is an adventure too: you have to buy them in person at Charing Cross, window 7 or 8 (even if you're taking the train from Victoria – if you try to buy the ticket there

now on the Eurasian landmass, you have your passport and a means of transport. There is, in principle, nothing to stop you cycling to Gibraltar, or Hyderabad, or Vladivostok, or Singapore... or just Calais, where you can enjoy a coffee and cake at a pavement cafe, and fill your panniers with two-euro bottles of supermarket vin de table and radioactive cheese. This is a ride that you can make as short and leisurely or as long and gruelling as you want it to be. Probably short and leisurely.

Dover to Calais is an experience – and it's cheap. You can get some great deals if you're travelling from London, tickets for combined train and ferry start at £33 for a five-day

they'll send you back to Charing Cross). You may also possibly be able to buy them over the phone (01227 450088). Reckon on around five hours from the time your train stumbles out of London to the time you freewheel off the ferry onto French concrete. From Dover Priory station it's signposted, about 2km to the port. Inside the port area, you have a couple of kilometres of scary hurtle over the concrete steppe of Dover Eastern Docks amid trucks and cars. You are waved through customs and eventually reach the check-in booths. After more LA-freeway scariness, some bee-people appear to shoo you up the ramp and into the ferry's belly. To secure your bike you'll spend a

roundabout follow signs to 'Centre ville'. On the way back, customs will show no interest in you; you can't get much wine and cheese in two panniers. They think.

■ Also in the area

Within a kilometre of leaving the ferry at Calais you'll be in a modern, rather characterless town square with a 'tower' (actually a heap of mud-coloured bricks) at its far corner. Here are a supermarket and shops to stock up on cheap wine and Camembert stamped with a half-life instead of an eat-by date. Plus plenty of cafes and bistros, and a postcard shop. If you turn left at the end of the square, that road takes you past the Tourist Info on your left and the railway station on your right. Beyond is the floral Town Hall, before which stands Rodin's sculpture of the legendary burghers of Calais, who offered to sacrifice themselves to save the townspeople a long time ago. As ever with Rodin, they seem to have awfully big feet. For Cape Town, Singapore, Vladivostok etc., carry on from here and ask for directions en-route.

while hunting in vain for a thicker rail and a piece of rope thinner than those available.

After you pass through customs at the other end, keep an eye on that fence to your right: as soon as it stops, get on to the foot/cycle-path and double back right, heading west. That will save you the couple of kilometres return trip out to the roundabout and back. On the way back you can't use this shortcut, unless you present yourself as a foot passenger. The road goes over a short bridge; at the

> *Fill your panniers with supermarket vin de table and radioactive cheese*

As for Dover, there's a mostly good seafront Sustrans route that runs from Dover to Folkestone one way, or anti-clockwise round the coast from Dover right up to London via Margate the other. *The Garden of England Cycle Route* is the map you

want. National Cycle Route 1 runs from Dover to the Shetland Islands, via London, Edinburgh and John O'Groats. National Cycle Route 2 runs from Dover to St Austell *(see page 38)* along the south coast.

Other places like this

There are lots of bike/ferry experiences from the rail-accessible ports of England and Wales. The Harwich-Hook of Holland ferry takes just three hours to steam across to the Netherlands. At the Hook you're right on the fabulous, traffic-free LF1, which takes you right up the Dutch coast: leisure cycling at its very best, and a must-do bike trip. It's ideal for a bank holiday weekend or a whole week, and suitable for families and even the most occasional cyclists.

The Hull-Zeebrugge ferry is an underrated gem for foreign cycling trips. The approach to the ship, along the shore of the Humber through docks and developments,

is interesting enough. Next morning, after your overnight trip, you're only 10km or so down a straight canal to beautiful Bruges (or 'Brugge', if you are Flemish, or if you enjoy the potential of anagrams). Book for a group of four in advance, and your fare is absurdly cheap (£60 return including cabins there and back).

Other options include: Holyhead-Dublin (which can also be ludicrously cheap if you take a late-train-and-ferry option); Harwich-Esbjerg or Cuxhaven; Newcastle-various Norwegian ports; Portsmouth-St Malo, Le Havre, Caen or Bilbao; Poole-Cherbourg; Plymouth-Roscoff or Santander; Fishguard-Rosslare. The Internet is the best place to research these.

Snackstop

Match supermarket, main square (Place d'Armes), Calais.
Across the square from the Café de la Tour, this is a handy place to stock up for a picnic or for stuff to take home.

Bevvy break

Café de la Tour, main square (Place d'Armes), Calais.
Right opposite la Tour (French for 'pile of rubble') in the square is this traditional bistro, black-tied waiters and all.

Quirkshop

Calais has several monuments to and a museum for crossings of la manche. The museum is near Cap Blanc Nez. Downhill from it is a statue to Hubert Latham (who failed to fly across in 1909). About 15km inland in the Forêt de Guînes, a pillar marks the first balloon crossing in 1785.

Tourer's tick list

✓ Rodin's sculpture in front of Calais Town Hall
✓ Cycle south from Calais alongside Canal de Guînes
✓ Cycle Opal Coast, west from Calais along roller-coaster D940

OS 179, grid ref TR335418
INFO www.seat61.com; Dover Visitor Information Centre, Old Town Gaol, Biggin St, Dover,
tel. 01304 205108, tic@doveruk.com

CHANNEL TUNNEL

WHERE *Underneath the English Channel*

WHAT *The Channel Tunnel*

WHY *Experience of taking your bike on Eurostar or the Shuttle*

HOW *Eurostar from St Pancras, or train to Folkestone for the Shuttle*

Ferries may well be the most atmospheric and leisurely way to take your bike with you on a trip overseas, but trains are quicker and more stylish – and you get to take your bike with you under the Channel Tunnel. There are two ways of doing this: by Eurostar from St Pancras to Paris, or by the special bike-trailer service on Le Shuttle from Folkestone to Calais.

Under the sea to Calais or Paris

You can take your bike on Eurostar trains, for £20 with prior booking, or without a booking, for free. The catch is that they must be in a bag and go through the X-ray machines, which means you'll have to take off the wheels, turn the handlebars, remove the saddle and rack... no problem with a folding bike, and quite possible with a road bike, but a lot of hassle with a touring bike. And then you have to cart the bag around with you.

The alternative is Eurotunnel Shuttle, Eurostar's parallel service for car drivers. They put you in a minibus and your bike on a trailer behind it, and then drive you into the Shuttle's steel python. It's all rather fun. You can't rely on it as a turn-up service, because they only take six bikes per minibus, and there are only two bike-minibuses per day from Folkestone, departing at 8am and 3.30pm from the excitingly named Eurotunnel Administration Building Car Park. (The return mini- buses from Calais leave the Centre d'Affaires next to the Marques Avenue design outlet at 12.30pm and 6pm). You'd best book in advance. So it needs a bit of setting up, but it's not expensive – only £32 return for adult with bike, and only £16 for a day return.

The tunnel is the second longest in the world at 50km, so being able to take your bike through it is something worth ticking off. (Only the Seikan – which links the islands of Honshu and Hokkaido in Japan by a rather underutilised railway line – is

longer, at 54km. We don't know if you can take bikes on their trains – let us know and we could put it in 50 Quirky Bike Rides around Japan...) You'll have to be up early if you want to catch the 8pm minibus departure – there's only one train from London that'll do you, the 5.30am from Charing Cross. The directions given on the Eurotunnel website for cyclists coming from Folkestone station are as follows: Alight at Folkestone West Station. Turn left out of the station onto Station Road. Follow the road round and

to do during the twenty-minute crossing; you're like loose change in those vacuum tubes that used to whizz up and down between cash desks of ancient department stores.

■ Also in the area

Sustrans' National Cycle Route 2 runs along the south coast, through Folkestone, takes in a lot of lovely promenade riding, and has some thrillingly chalky scenery. Hythe is just up the way, for the Romney Hythe & Dymchurch Railway *(see page 50)* and you're not far from Dover in case you prefer the ferry *(see page 38)*.

turn left into Cheriton Road. Follow Cheriton Road until you come to the garage on your right. Take the road off to the left, opposite the garage towards Tesco. Carry on along this road, over the traffic lights, passing the Tesco garage on your right. The Eurotunnel Administration Building will be on your left. Turn left into the visitor's car park, the Cycle Service pick-up point is located behind the building.

Taking the Shuttle is a mix of the fascinating and the tedious. You join a line of traffic which slides down a slipway onto one of many platforms in the sprawling mar-shalling yards at Folkestone. Your minibus drives onto one of the big boxy carriages through a side panel, the doors shut, and the inscrutable giant worm burrows its way underground. There's not much

To the west of Calais, the Opal Coast offers a spectacular, if hilly, ride to Boulogne along the D940 coast road. You have fabulous views of the Channel, and the road dips and rises through some pretty villages. Calais to Wimereux and back makes a good day trip. If you want something flatter, you can go south out of Calais town centre along the Canal de Guînes through quiet farming country and small towns. Come off the canal route at a fork and take the D127 to the pleasant town of Guînes itself, which has a forest worth exploring nearby. Or stay on the canal all the way to Watten, about 30km away; from here you can ride to Ardres and rejoin a spur of the canal which takes you back to Calais. The good news for those with a ferry to

The Channel Tunnel is the second longest in the world

catch is that there isn't really much to detain you in Calais once you've seen the Town Square.

■ Other places like this

Actually, you don't have to go abroad to experience the bus-shuttle thing, or even pay any money. The massively-trafficked Dartford Crossing, east of London, is a tunnel-bridge system that allows the M25 to cross the Thames, though it's called the A282, not the M25, for that short stretch. Southbound traffic takes the bridge, northbound traffic the tunnels. Neither bridge nor tunnel allows bicycles, but there are free bus shuttles to take you and your bike across in both directions.

Cyclists are prohibited from riding across the bridge or through the tunnels, as the website, www.dartfordrivercrossing.co.uk, says. However the Crossing staff will be pleased to arrange for cyclists to be transported from one side to the other. Northbound cyclists should follow the cycle paths provided to the sign 'Cyclists Wait Here'. From this point forward free transport will be provided to carry you and your bike through the Tunnels. Southbound cyclists should dismount at the Essex Control building and wait for free transfer across the QE2 Bridge. A free call telephone is provided should this point be unattended. If you are riding a tandem or travelling as a group e.g. a cycle club, it is advisable to make prior arrangements by contacting the Crossing. The transfer should take between 15-30 minutes (the contact number for the crossing is 01322 221603).

Snackstop
(Cafes, various) The villages of Audresselles, Audinghen and Wissant (halfway between Calais and Wimereux, which makes a nice day trip) are replete with cafes and bars.

Bevvy break
Being France, food and drink go together, so see above.

Quirkshop
By the entrance to the tunnel in Folkestone, and hence the last or first thing you see in England, is a white horse outline on the hillside to the north. Unlike the other white horses on hillsides around England (see page 32) this one isn't cut into the chalk, but consists of white slabs. It was laid down in 2003. The best place to see it is from Cheriton, just west of Folkestone, 1km south of the figure.

Tourer's tick list
✓ Folkestone White Horse
✓ Canal de Guînes
✓ Rodins by Calais town hall
✓ Cheap wine, cheese etc

OS 179, grid ref TR186376
INFO www.eurotunnel.com;
ticket reservations, 01303 282201

EYNSFORD

WHERE   *Eynsford, Kent*

WHAT   *Kent village lanes, a ride of 10km-20km*

WHY   *Splash through England's most picturesque village ford*

HOW   *Train to Eynsford*

This ride through scenic, sometimes hilly, back lanes between pretty villages of commuter-belt Kent can be as long as you want. But it starts and ends in Eynsford, a pleasant little village in the Darent Valley that's home to what we rate as the country's best cycling ford.

Picturesque village watersplash par excellence of Kent

Why best? Because it's deep enough to be an exciting splash, a challenge to the mildly adventurous, but presenting no danger except dampened pride to the inexpert; because it has a quaint bridge alternative; because it's in an unmatched village setting; and because it's right next to village shops and inns where you can dry out on a warm summer afternoon. Eynsford, under an hour's train ride from London, is a delight for the pedalling paddler. It's a charming village, with four pubs, a restaurant and tea room, which in our judgment is about the right ratio. The ford over the River Darent is right in the middle of the place.

One possible circular route is as follows. From Eynsford station, head to the main road and turn left/south, branching off right soon after and going down a very steep hill. You're following a roughly square route through Well Hill and Crockenhill back to Eynsford (10km). If you're up for a bit more biking, strike north along the Darent Valley on the lanes through unspoilt Farningham, Horton Kirby, Darent and back (another 10km).

Another way of getting to Eynsford from London is to follow the Thames Path (part of the National Cycle Route 1) all the way along the south bank to Dartford and cycle 14km or so on roads to Eynsford, taking the train back.

Eynsford village is a kilometre freewheel down the hill from the station. The ford is on your left as you enter the village. It's picture-postcard stuff, and on a warm day the temptation to dip your wheels will be irresistible. But be warned that the apparently convincing depth gauge does not quite reflect reality out in the middle. To get a better feel for how much of your bike the fish will be able to inspect, your best bet is to wait for a lorry.

They are too wide for the old arched bridge alongside and slosh through the ford. Judge the depth from that.

One thing is for certain: you'll want to try splashing your way through. Because once a cyclist spots a ford, on the map or on the ground, an irresistible force tells us to go and cycle through it. Maybe it's an echo of that childhood delight for puddle-jumping in red wellies.

And if you mention fords to any group of cyclists, you'll find that everyone has their own anecdote. They fall into two types. First is 'How I fell off'. For maximum effect

this involves a dash of overenthusiasm, a crowd of amused onlookers, and some sort of deliquescent aftermath. Second is 'When we were little', a sepia-toned memory of a slosh in dad's old Austin in some elusive villagey location.

Well, in Eynsford, you can add another story to your collection.

Also in the area

Within a kilometre of the village are the remains of Eynsford's 11th-century castle; Lullingstone Castle, a historic manor house with large grounds; and (up a brief hill) a bird of prey centre, Eagle Heights. It's pleasant country to explore, and you can follow your nose – but you need a map to find your way back through the maze of twisting lanes.

The area south of here, towards Sevenoaks, is hilly and wooded with fabulous views from its many back lanes, but it's quite tough going. You're never far from a station, though.

Strike north from Eynsford 14km or so and you can join a lovely Sustrans

Route, the Garden of England. It takes you 300km from London to Folkestone, roughly following the coast clockwise and passing through Canterbury. Eynsford's train connections can easily hook you up with the Gardens route .

Other places like this

You don't have to go far in Britain to find a ford. We're submerged in them, as a glance at the website www.wetroads.co.uk will show: it lists over 1,700.

Tarr Steps, in deepest Somerset (OS 181, grid ref SS867321), is something special *(both pictures above)*. A minor road in middle of nowhere (a nowhere called Exmoor) crosses the often deepish and fastish River Barle via the famous ford. It's great to do on a mountain bike. If the river's in spate or you just don't fancy the crossing, use the 3000 year old bridge alongside – the 'Tarr Steps' of the title. It's a no-nonsense stack of stone slabs, as if commissioned from neolithic archi-

The apparently convincing depth gauge does not quite reflect reality out in the middle

tects in Stonehenge chic. You might have trouble cycling across it, it may be best to push your bike over the stone way and watch in hope in case any cars unwisely try to cross the river in full flow. Good news: there's a pub right by the bridge. Bad news: Tarr Steps is a long way from public transport. You can get most of the way there from Tiverton Parkway by cycling along Sustrans' West Country Way, but it's nearly 50km from the station.

In Tissington, Derbyshire (OS 119, grid ref SK199521) there's a splendid ford near the Tissington Trail, which is deservedly lauded as a flat, scenic, easy-peasy tourer's goodie *(see page 138)*. If you want to test your rugged bike on a warm day, and the moisture- repelling quality of your Ortlieb panniers, then just off the trail is this challenging, top quality immersion.

The Lôn Las Cymru, or Welsh National Cycle Route, offers a battery of water crossings. One of its alternative sections − 35km of lonely, wild, wonderful rough stuff between Llanwrtyd Wells and Pontrhydfendigaid − offers ford fans at least 16. MTBs and experienced navigators only, though: know how to use a compass, take a bearing, and cope with 17-letter place names.

Snackstop
Old Ford Cafe, Eynsford. *If you need warming up after getting wetter than you expected, this couldn't be closer.*

Bevvy break
Plough and Harrow, Riverside, Eynsham. *Decent pub within splashing distance of the ford, with outside tables so you can dry out in the summer sun. Real ale, food etc.*

Quirkshop
Eynsford village was home to 1920s composers Peter Warlock (who wrote the Capriol Suite) and EJ Moeran. They lived part of the time in a cottage here (on the way to the castle; it's marked with a plaque) and the rest of the time in Eynsford's pubs, getting as sloshed as the lorries tackling the village ford.

Tourer's tick list
✓ Bird of prey centre
✓ Castle and Roman villa in village
✓ Cycle under the railway viaduct
✓ Thames path

OS 177, grid ref TQ540655
INFO Swanley Library and Information Centre, London Road, Swanley BR8 7AE, tel. 01322 614660,
touristinfo @ swanley.org.uk

ROMNEY, HYTHE & DYMCHURCH RAILWAY

ROMNEY HYTHE & DYMCHURCH

WHERE   *Folkestone, Kent, to Rye, E Sussex (30km and train ride)*

WHAT   *Fascinatingly varied, flat coastal ride partly by train*

WHY   *Take your bike on an amazing miniature train*

HOW   *Train to Folkestone, train back from Rye*

This is a delightful, historic and scenic day trip that includes one of the oddest bike-friendly train rides in the world. Start from Folkestone, and cycle west along the Sustrans promenade route to Hythe station, by a canal. Here's where you catch your train. The Romney, Hythe & Dymchurch Railway (RH&DR), runs 23km from Hythe to Dungeness on the Kent coast and is the world's smallest passenger railway. Or perhaps the world's biggest train set.

Feel 12 feet tall as you and bike ride a miniature train

When you shoehorn your bike into the dwarf guard's-van, you're a four-metre tall circus freak with a machine the size of a penny-farthing. Captain Jack Howey knew all about such dreams of grandeur: a racing driver and a millionaire landowner, he had the railway built in 1927.

The locals say that he fitted his Rolls with train wheels to drive it along the railway – unmarked crossings and all – at 100kph. It became instantly popular and, after a colourful history including requisition in wartime, now serves as both a tourist attraction, (with services hourly in summer, occasional for the rest of the year) and a community facility. It ferries kids to school in term-time, maybe the last UK generation who want to be engine drivers when they grow up. The locomotives and carriages look as though they want to be real trains when they grow up, too.

The very charm of the RH&DR is that everything is small but perfectly formed: take a picture without people and you'd think it was a standard gauge heritage railway. It's only when people intrude that your sense of proportion is knocked out of proportion. Hythe to Dungeness is £10.90 return, with bikes 50p extra, which is pretty good value for an entire carriage. If you have high-rise handlebars your bike may simply not fit, and if you have a tandem, it could be easier for you to simply hitch the guard's van to the back and tow it yourself.

The trains scoot along at a top speed of 40kph, which feels a lot faster than it sounds (you'd hardly even notice that speed if you were doing it freewheeling downhill). There's an observation car, which somehow manages to have a licensed bar inside it. Normal-sized cafes are available at Hythe, New Romney and Dungeness stations. The terminus at Dungeness has a 'balloon loop' so the train can do a uey for its return trip. You can cycle back to Hythe along a Sustrans route, but it's inland on roads. You may prefer to go back by train or to continue to Rye.

But first, Dungeness is a curious little area to explore by bike. It has an unusual 'village' of huts and a pub, dispersed around its rather untidy expanse of shingle. They're haphazardly arranged, as if dropped by a cargo plane from a great

height. Some have put up colourful installations of found objects such as plastic spades, Wellington boots and plates. The shingle bank is one of the largest such examples in the world, which adds something timeless and powerful to the atmosphere. As does the nuclear power station looming next door to Dymchurch station.

if you have a tandem, you could tow the guard's van yourself

From here you can cycle along the signposted Sustrans route. Dull flat minor roads inland take you to Lydd, then Camber where you rejoin the coast, and go on to historic Rye *(see page 50)*, which has a cobbley charm. You can take the train back home from here.

■ Also in the area

The shingle area round Dungeness is home to a remarkable range of exotic forms of life, some of whom own the seaside-retreat shacks you see dotted around it. The steps to the top of the black-and-white lighthouse give you a bird's-eye view. You can see why the place attracts arty and alternative types: it's windswept, individual, and unconventionally attractive – you'll find little bits of candy-coloured vegetation that you've never seen before growing in the sharp stone dunes, and all kinds of moths, butterflies and spiders.

One third of all the varieties of flora in the UK can be found here, which isn't bad for a load of pebbles. Dungeness's most famous resident was the artist, poet, film maker and gay rights activist Derek Jarman (1942-94). In 1986 he moved to Prospect Cottage, one of the shingle bank's many wooden huts. The beach garden he made from local materials has been the subject of several books, and is still there to be seen today. The cottage is something of a pilgrimage site, and you might see couples by the cottage, enthusiastically discussing his oeuvre.

Folkestone is on Sustrans' Garden of England route, which winds round the coast via Canterbury to London. The other way, National Cycle Route 2 goes beyond Rye to Winchelsea (another one of the Cinque Ports, of which there are either seven, 14 or nearly 40, depending on how you count them) and ultimately Hastings.

■ Other places like this

There are at least two other miniature railways like the RH&DR –

specifically 15-inch (38cm) gauge lines which run regular, scheduled services and carry bicycles – though the RH&DR is the longest and, we think, the best. It was Howey's failure to buy the Ravenglass and Eskdale Railway (R&E), another miniature service up on the south-western edge of the Lake District, that led to his building the RH&DR as an alternative. The R&E (www.ravenglass-railway.co.uk) runs through lovely scenery from Eskdale, near Boot on the Hardknott Pass *(see page 153)*, to Ravenglass on the coast. There you can join the main rail line, and this can be neatly combined with the cardiac challenge of a crossing of Hardknott Pass, and some further opportunities for two-wheeled Lakes malarkey.

The Bure Valley Railway (BVRW) runs through pleasant countryside from Wroxham to Aylsham in Norfolk, and gladly takes bikes for £2.50 extra. You can cycle alongside the track, which makes the logistics of planning a return trip reasonably straightforward. Wroxham station, north-east of Norwich, also has main line services. Bike hire is available at Hoveton, near Wroxham – see the BVRW website (www.bvrw.co.uk) for details.

A little further north, on the north Norfolk coast, the microscopic Wells Harbour railway (www.whr.cjb.net), on a knife-edge 10 1/2-inch (16cm) gauge, and doesn't normally take bikes, yet one of us managed to do so after a calamitous puncture. But, as always, it helps if you ask nicely, and look attractive and female.

Snackstop

Seafood stall. *Enjoy an excellent little pot of mixed frutti di mare – prawns, whelks, cuttlefish, squid, cockles and mussels dead, dead-O – for a quid from the seafood-stall shed just by the level crossing just before Dungeness. There are cafes in New Romney, Hythe and Dungeness stations, and they all have picnic tables.*

Bevvy break

The Britannia, Dungeness. *Between the two lighthouses is this Shepherd Neame pub (love their beer, hate their ads). Beach opposite pub, outside tables. Fresh local fish.*

Quirkshop

Dungeness crabs are not named after this Dungeness, but one in the US, whose existence is mildly unsettling.

Tourer's tick list

✓ Rye
✓ Dip in sea (if warm enough)
✓ Derek Jarman's Prospect Cottage, Dungeness

OS 189, grid ref TR153348
INFO Hythe Tourist Information, En Route, Red Lion Sq, Hythe, Kent CT21 5AZ, tel. 01303 267799, hvc@entoure.co.uk; train timetables, info 01797 365353

WELLINGTON ARCH

WHERE *London, Westminster to Hyde Park (5km one way)*

WHAT *Mostly park riding, past all the tourist must-sees*

WHY *London sights from the saddle, and the unique passage through Wellington Arch*

HOW *Train to Waterloo or Paddington*

Cycling from the London Eye and the Houses of Parliament, past Buckingham Palace, and along through Hyde Park is one of the world's greatest sightseeing cycle rides. And en route you do something no other great city can offer: a car-free cycle under the huge triumphal Wellington Arch.

The world's most atmospheric cycle-commute

Start from Westminster Bridge (Waterloo station is close by; you can also arrive by tube on the Circle Line, *(see page 70)*; or get here via the Thames Path, *(see page 58)*. Enjoy the splendid views of the Eye, and of tourists snapping Big Ben's Clock Tower on their mobiles. If it's rush hour you'll already be part of a steady stream of lemon-jacketed pedalling commuters. Watch your back in the traffic round Parliament Square (you may prefer to walk this bit) and head up Birdcage Walk past St James's Park. Jag right then left past the car-free front of Buckingham Palace, up Constitution Hill. (There is no hill here, but then neither does Britain have a constitution.) Green Park is on your right, with a cycle path alternative just by the road. The splendid Arch looms ahead. Rush hour is the best time to do this, because you'll be part of a commuting peloton with professional London in all its two-wheeled forms: snappy folders, beat-up old bangers, paperweight road bikes,

even the odd recumbent. (Cycle-commuting is up 80% in the last couple of years – no congestion charge, it's door-to-door, cheaper than public transport, faster and more reliable.)

Triumphal Arches are show-off gateways to nowhere, the gossip-mag celebs of the monument world: self-regarding, serving no obvious purpose, famous for being famous, simply there to be looked at. And London's is rare if not unique because you can cycle through it, traffic-free in fact, which isn't the case with the Arc de Triomphe or Brandenburg Gate, say. The Arch is in the middle of a roundabout on a motor-free cycle plaza occupied by the arch, some garden, and a few discreet and dignified war memorials. The impeccable gravel surface is even and clean, and creamy white as a Barbados beach, complemented by the bronze of fresh horse manure, so watch out: riders frequently use this route (there are even special horse-shaped traffic

Spend some time here: have a picnic; buy a coffee; watch the skaters doing their slalom tricks with plastic cups; circumnavigate the Serpentine; try to find the unpreposessing Diana Memorial.

■ Also in the area

Want to see even more of those famous stock-footage sights used by foreign TV news report to denote 'London'? The Arch can be part of a longer route that includes plenty more, on a route mostly off-road. If you start from Tower Bridge over in the east, you cycle all along the south bank of the Thames (past Tate Modern, the South Bank, the Eye) to get to Westminster Bridge. You can also approach Westminster Bridge from the west along the Thames Path

lights at the crossing, next to the cycle-shaped ones).

The Arch is open to the public, and you can go up inside to the top for fine views down to Buckingham Palace and over Hyde Park. Finished in 1830, the Arch was planned to celebrate victory in the Napoleonic wars. In 1883 it was moved a short distance to its present location, thanks to the vic-

Triumphal arches are the gossip-mag celebs of the monument world

tory of a force even greater than an Imperial Army: a road widening scheme. The statue on the top dates from 1912 and scarily depicts the angel of peace.

At the far end, most cyclists bound for Hyde Park make a short-cut to Marble Arch instead of two separate crossings to their left; if you're a crowd-follower, make sure you're not at the tail end of the fast-track group, they tend to cut it a bit fine. Once in Hyde Park, you have traffic-free paths either west (the Albert Hall is at the far end) or north (to Paddington or Oxford St).

(from Reading or even Bristol if you're really keen).

Carry on a kilometre west through Hyde Park along the cycle paths, and you reach the Albert Memorial, with the Albert Hall opposite. That's next door to the Science Museum and Natural History Museum.

In addition to the Thames paths, there are several canal towpath rides which thread you through capital traffic-free, with plenty more sights en route *(see pages 66 and 74)*.

Transport for London produce

very useful free cycle maps for the capital. Essentially, they're A to Z maps with cycle routes marked on (you can also find them on the web at www.tfl.gov.uk/cycles/routes/london-cycleguides.asp). They're also handed out free in many London cycle shops. Anyone who regularly cycles in London will want to be part of the London Cycle Campaign (see www.lcc.org.uk).

■ Other places like this

London itself offers three other arch-cycling experiences. Adjacent to Wellington Arch, you can cycle under the impressive entrance to Hyde Park. Britain's other triumphal arch – Marble Arch itself, originally the entrance to Buckingham Palace – is a kilometre beyond, at the north-east corner of Hyde Park, by Speaker's Corner. You can cycle under it, kind of, but it's in a traffic island and not connected to a sensible route so there's not an obvious point.

Admiralty Arch however, at the south end of Trafalgar Square, is nearby and almost as thrilling as Wellington. You share the road through it, though – with impatient taxis, or with logjams of car drivers, all complaining about the traffic. Charing Cross, a stone's throw from Trafalgar Square, is the point to which all distances to London are measured.

Outside London, Lincoln's Newport Arch is said to be the only surviving Roman arch with a road passing underneath *(see page 121)*. Further up in cycle-friendly York, entry into the town centre is through bike/pedestrian arches in the old city walls.

If it's the mass-commuting experience you're after – being part of a throng of bikes off to work, Beijing-style – then nowhere beats Cambridge for sheer abundance of cyclists *(see page 86)*.

Snackstop
Lido Cafe, Hyde Park. *West from the Arch, in Hyde Park. Touristy but pleasant with outdoor terrace by Serpentine.*

Bevvy break
The Grenadier, Old Barrack Yard, Wilton Row, SW1. *Just south-west of the arch, remarkable and historic little pub.*

Quirkshop
Wellington Arch seems to be the regular venue for the World Naked Bike Ride, annual since 2004. A few hundred riders strip off on a June Saturday and trundle around town.
See www.worldnakedbikeride.org.

Tourer's tick list
✓ Buckingham Palace
✓ Houses of Parliament
✓ Trafalgar Square
✓ Hyde Park
✓ Albert Hall
✓ Kensington museums

OS 176, grid ref TQ285799
INFO www.english-heritage.org.uk

LONDON'S LOMBARD ST

WHERE *London: Tower Bridge to Greenwich and back (16km round trip)*

WHAT *Mostly traffic-free river- and waterside paths*

WHY *Great London sights, and England's bendiest bike path*

HOW *Train to Tower Bridge or Tube to Tower Hill*

This flat, leisurely, car-free, waterside trail through redeveloped docks areas is a sightseer's delight. It includes London's answer to Lombard St ("the crookedest street in the world") in San Francisco. It's an absolutely fabulous, very varied ride: relaxing, easy, full of quirky stuff ancient and modern, and offers some spectacular views.

Dockside delight, and London's answer to San Francisco

Start from Tower Bridge. The Bridge is exciting to cycle across, with the vague suggestion of staring down the oesophagus of some fabulous monster. But it's also narrow and a bit hairy. If you feel harassed by all the buses, you can walk your bike across on one of the wide footpaths at the side. Watching the bridge go up to allow a ship or tall boat to pass underneath is well worthwhile (upcoming lift times are posted at www. towerbridge.org.uk). From the Bridge's north side, double back down the lane on your right: St Katharine's Way, immediately east of the bridge approach road. Explore the touristy St Katharine's Dock area. Bombed to bits in World War II, it's now luxury apartments, cafes and shops, and a posh marina.

Cycle over the small lifting bridge beyond the underpass. Go about 200m to a junction, just beyond it take a left to cycle alongside a basin covered in pondweed. An Ornamental Canal 200m or so beyond that, reached by a zig-zag descent: London's 'Lombard St'. The original is in San Francisco, and is a steep and picturesque descent of eight road hairpins that wind the traffic down through gushing floral displays. Though its tag has always been "the crookedest street in the world", it isn't even the crookedest in San Francisco. Vermont St has seven steeper and tighter bends; and the crookedest in the world is Wall St, of course. But here you are in London, on a nicer and calmer bike path, free of 4x4s and gawping

tourists. Not quite the plummet of San Fran's runny tourist honeypot, but still too brisk and bendy to reach the bottom without brakes.

Carry on along the 'towpath' (from which nothing has ever been towed: it's an ornamental canal). There's a trim newbuild Dutch feel to the place. Go over a hillock and through another basin to join the Thames Path. Go east (left) along the riverside towards Docklands.

On a weekday, Docklands bustles with financial people multi-tasking. They can walk, talk to a colleague, text their partner, listen to their iPod, and step out in front of you, all at the same time. Carry on, with the river always on your right, to Greenwich foot tunnel. Cross under the river using the foot-tunnel *(see page 63)* to Greenwich. By bike, the Naval College is best appreciated by riding along the riverside path on the south bank, a little bit east from the tunnel. Inside its grounds, you can wheel your bike (and probably hear Trinity College's musicians practising Bach), but you're not allowed to cycle.

From Greenwich you can follow the Thames Path along the river's

■ Also in the area

In Greenwich, ride a few hundred metres up the car-free lane to the Observatory. You'll see it on the top of the hill in the park above the town. There are great views from here, and the freewheel back down to the town is fun. The Thames path continues east from here right along the riverside, with the old-and-new panorama of Canary Wharf on one side, the Royal Naval College on the other, and the sleeping hedgehog of the 02 dome over to the east.

On the north-western edge of Canary Wharf, there's a roundabout at Heron Quays festooned with dozens of traffic lights, all pointing in different directions. It's an artwork ('Traffic Light Tree'): they used to all flash red, amber and green chaotically, confusing the hell out of visitors, especially as there are real, normal traffic lights hidden in the middle of them all. Sadly though the artwork's lights seem to be turned off nowadays.

south bank, mostly traffic-free and alongside the Thames, all the way back to Tower Bridge. En-route you'll see a life-size statue of Peter the Great. For someone two metres tall, he apparently had a very small head. If you fancy going back to central London from Greenwich in style, you can take your bike on the ferry shuttles, but the ride back is pleasant and well worth doing.

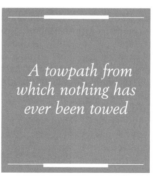

A towpath from which nothing has ever been towed

Up for a really long ride? Keep cycling along the Thames's south side, you can go on Sustrans bike paths all the way to Dover by going east (National Cycle Route 1), or Bristol by going west (National Cycle Route 4).

You can combine this route with other London rides in the book *(see pages 62, 66 and 74)*.

■ Other places like this

If you're looking for on-road recreational zig-zagging, then the bendiest road in Britain, according to a 'study' (i.e. 'PR stunt', concocted by Continental Tyres in 2006), is the B3081 between Cann Common and Tollard Hill, Dorset. At one point in its tortuous progress, Zig Zag Hill, there are between four and seven hairpins dropping 50m, depending on your feelings about cornering coiffure.

Continental's website mixes imperial and metric measurements rather charmingly, and notes that it scored a whopping 352 kilonewton-seconds of lateral force-impulse in a steady 30mph descent (www. conti-online.com). The survey's next bendiest roads were the A686 between Penrith and Melmerby, Cumbria: the A537 between Macclesfield and Buxton, Cheshire/Derbyshire: the A466 between Monmouth and Staunton, Monmouth: the A4061 between Pricetown and Treorchy, Rhondda.

After that come the B2130 (between Godalming and Cranleigh, Surrey), the B6270 (between Keld and Reeth, Yorkshire), and the A39 (between Bridgwater and Minehead, Somerset).

Perhaps surprisingly the bendiest Scottish road, the B797 (between Mennock and Warnlockhead, Dumfries and Galloway), only makes No. 10; maybe they're just better engineers.

Snackstop
Picnic. *Stock up at Waitrose in Thomas More St, on the east edge off St Katharine's Dock, and find a sunny bench.*

Bevvy break
Dickens Inn. *A touristy contraption, large and loud, but a very pleasant place for an al fresco pint.*

Quirkshop
If you're at the south side of Tower Bridge very early on a Friday morning, Bermondsey market (about a kilometre south) runs from 4am to noon. Why so early? Because until it was repealed in 2003, under an obscure law called marché ouvert, stolen goods could be sold here with impunity as long as it's before sunrise. I never found any of my nicked bikes.

Tourer's tick list
✓ The Tower
✓ Bermondsey market
✓ Thames, Canary Wharf, Dome views
✓ Traffic light tree
✓ Canalside cycling
✓ Greenwich

OS 177, grid ref TQ343803
INFO City Information Centre, St Paul's Churchyard, London EC4M 8BX, tel. 0207 332 1456, www.cityoflondon.gov.uk

WOOLWICH FERRY

WHERE *London: Greenwich to Woolwich and back (18km round trip)*

WHAT *Mostly traffic-free river- and waterside paths*

WHY *Great London sights, and England's only free ferry*

HOW *Train to Greenwich*

his is another delightful, car-free waterside day ride, one of England's best and easiest townscape day rides. It goes past some of the most remarkable sights of the capital you can experience from the saddle, including two tunnels, the Dome, an airport, a hemisphere crossing – and a unique free ferry.

Amazing riverside cityscapes, and a free ferry

Start from Greenwich, and take the foot tunnel under the river to the north bank. You take your bike down in a wooden-panelled lift that resembles an Edwardian drawing room. Push your bike in the tunnel itself or they might not let you use the lift at the other end, and there are a lot of stairs. Follow bike route signs north through the shiny business newbuild of Docklands, and past Billingsgate Fish Market head east. The bike path takes you on the bridge over the River Lea with sweeping views of the O2 dome. Signposting isn't great after this: you need to jag right along Dock Road and then duck left under the main road to head east into Royal Victoria Dock. There's the slightly unbelievable sight of a beach here. Head east along the north side of the dock, past ExCel and a floating hotel, watching the planes gliding down into London City Airport. At the east end of the dock, turn south under the main road that looks like a bridge. The Airport is on your left, but you head east along Factory Road to Woolwich Ferry.

Ferries by bike are something special. The only disadvantage is the cost. There is no such thing as a free launch. But here at Woolwich, the five-minute shuttle crossing of the Thames is – like the NHS, hotel toiletries, and cycling itself – free at the point of use. It also just happens to be the link from the north to south bank. But hurry: the boat may only be operating until 2013, if and when the proposed Thames

Gateway Bridge nearby is completed. The ferry (two boats on weekdays, one at weekends) runs every ten minutes (15 minutes at weekends) from 6am to 8pm. It's a proper, chunky affair, built for 500 passengers and 200 tonnes of vehicles. A ferry service has been operating here since 1889, and for free because it's the aquatic link between the North Circular and South Circular roads. The short approaches have queues of cars, lorries with CLEAN ME fingered into their grime, and the odd bus.

Bikes can head straight to the front of the road queue, and be first on the car deck when the boat docks. If you join the ferry with the foot passengers, you'll have to schlepp your bike up and down some stairs. The car deck also has better views. Most drivers don't bother to get out of their vehicles during the crossing, but you and bike can get a good all-round view of the riverscape. It can be quite sociable as there'll be a fair old mix of tourists taking snaps, nonchalant locals and drivers impatient to get stuck into the next queue. Downstairs, it looks much like a ferry: a maze of metal doors and portals to empty rooms marked No Entry, boxes of mystery equipment, and framed lists of ancient regulations in microscopic type.

At times when the ferry isn't operating, or just for something different, there is a foot tunnel just downstream, similar to Greenwich's (but slightly longer, at 500m). Look

the three skyscrapers in Docklands (HSBC, Citigroup, and 'Canary Wharf' or 1 Canada Square) appear to swop places as your river path winds round, slyly changing your perspective. A large circuit around the O2 Dome and a stretch through desolate factories brings you back to Greenwich.

■ Also in the area

A few hundred metres uphill from where the ferry docks in South Woolwich is the old Arsenal (which is where the football team came from). There are a few quirky statues not by Antony Gormley, and the artillery museum, Firepower, which has a decent cafe. If you want to head east from the Ferry along the Thames Path, the south bank takes you almost immediately into what feels like countryside – London appears to stop abruptly. Eventually it takes you to Dartford, and (now called Garden of England Route by Sustrans) will take you Canterbury and Dover if you wish.

for a pointy, round brick hut.

Ride back along the Thames Path, on the river's south bank, all the way to Greenwich. It's almost all off-road and water-side. You go past the amazing flood defence of the Thames Barrier, whose shiny metal pods look unsettlingly like alien landing craft.

All this plus two tunnels, the Dome, an airport, and a hemisphere crossing

Looking upriver it's quite a surprise to see that the Millennium Dome appears to be on the north side of the river, thanks to a trick of the estuary's Escher-like perspectives. Another optical illusion makes

The Woolwich to Greenwich route along the south bank of the Thames is National Cycle Route 1, which links Dover to John O'Groats.

In Greenwich you might want to cycle up the hill to the observatory, from where you can get one of the best views of the sashaying London riverscape. You can also cycle from eastern to western hemisphere here, across the merid-

ian line as displayed in the observatory forecourt apparently has shifted a hundred metres or so east, into the parkland.

Just north of the northern end of Greenwich foot tunnel, Mudchute City Farm is a good place for families, and offers the sight of fields of cows with the skyscrapers of Canary Wharf in the background.

Woolwich's ten-minute shuttle: it sails overnight to Zeebrugge or Rotterdam.

There are a handful of big-city ferries that shuttle cyclists across estuaries, notably in Liverpool *(see page 154)*, as well as lots of very small services *(see page 81)*. But Woolwich is the only free ferry of any size in the country.

■ Other places like this

For big-city waterside rides, giving a mix of old and new docklands, see the Mersey Ferry entry *(page 154)* or the Humber Bridge entry *(page 158)*. The route from Hull city centre along the river, through the docks out east to the ferry terminal at King George Dock, offers some remarkable sights including a tidal barrier of its own, the world's biggest fishtank, *The Deep,* (shaped like a shark), and wide views of the purple, acned Humber. The ferry from King George Dock though goes a bit further than

Snackstop
Firepower Cafe, Royal Arsenal, Woolwich. *Decently priced with real coffee, gourmet sandwiches and cakes. The Arsenal riverside area is OK for a picnic on a warm day.*

Bevvy break
The Prince Albert (Rose's), Hare St, Woolwich. *Traditional no-nonsense pub with good real ale, on a pedestrian street one minute from the ferry.*

Quirkshop
London City Airport is worth a visit, if only because there aren't many airports that you'd visit by bike. Its tiny size – you can park a few metres from the entrance – makes it quite charming. If you want a coffee while you're here, bring a credit card.

Tourer's tick list
✓ Futurama cityscape of docks
✓ Two tunnels
✓ Riverside path
✓ Greenwich Observatory
✓ Thames Barrier

OS 177, grid ref TQ432794
INFO Greenwich Tourist Information, Pepys House, 2 Cutty Sark Gardens, Greenwich SE10 9SLW, tel. 0870 6082000, tic@greenwich.gov.uk

NORTH CIRCULAR ROAD

WHERE *London: Paddington Station to Southall (20km)*

WHAT *Canal towpath*

WHY *Tranquil London backwater, and bizarre flight over main road*

HOW *Train to Paddington (return by train from Southall)*

his flat, easy-going, surprisingly tranquil car-free route through the backwaters of North London also lets you perform the miracle of flying over the North Circular road on your bike. The Grand Union Canal (Paddington Arm) threads its way west from just behind the mainline station to bustling Southall, where you can hop on a train back – a lovely day ride.

An amazing aqueduct over the North Circular

Starting out from Paddington station, turn left and cycle northish alongside the eastish side of the station, which leads to the canal. There's an oddity here just a hundred metres or so from the station. As Milton Keynes has concrete cows, London has concrete commuters. Right here on the towpath, two bored-looking chaps, casually dressed, stand like statues – and that's because they are statues. You can take an amusing picture of one of them holding your bike. Carry on through Little Venice. You're not supposed to cycle for a stretch of a kilometre or so, though people do.

From here it's smooth and tranquil paved towpath. You pass a large supermarket and a coffee shop, which is handy for toilets. About 9km out of Paddington, the eyelid-like gossamer framework of Wembley Stadium is far to the right, followed by a less graceful Travelodge on your left.

The aqueduct comes as quite a surprise after the gentle backdoor waterscape of small factories, railway sidings, residential estates, and almost-rural linear greenery. Suddenly, it thrusts over a concrete aqueduct – several stories high – with eight lanes of traffic scraping the North Circular. The first aqueduct was built to carry the canal here in 1933, and was upgraded in the early 1990s to the curious two-lane affair that bestrides the A406 today. In the middle of the aqueduct is a concrete island with two pillars, each bearing the Middlesex

coat-of-arms. Just beyond the A406 crossing, hidden behind shrubby trees, is an old aqueduct over the River Brent (as in '-ford') dating from 1801.

Carry on another 10km or so along the towpath. It's mostly unpaved, but OK even in wet weather. Take a left off the canal and go a kilometre or so into bustling Southall, whose High Street is much more like India that west London. (If you come to a canal junction, you've gone about 2km too far.) Here you can eat fabulously and cheaply from all over the subcontinent, buy delicious honey mangoes from Pakistan and a bargain sari, and snap up some Hindi pop CDs. You can also catch a train from Southall station and be back in Paddington in 20 minutes, or retrace your steps – if your bottom is up to it.

■ Also in the area...

Paddington Station is just north of Hyde Park, which is a splendid car-free (or at least car-light) place to explore by bike. There are traffic-free paths round the Serpentine and along the north and east sides of the park. From the south-east corner of the park, Buckingham Palace and the Houses of Parliament are next door.

About 3km along the canal from Paddington, where the supermarket and Starbucks are, you're just a little to the north of Notting Hill. You might just spot Madonna or David Cameron on their bikes (not illustrated) somewhere round here.

This arm of the Grand Union Canal joins the main branch at Bulls Bridge, just south of Southall. A right turn here (west) will follow the main line of the Grand Union most of the way for the 200km to Birmingham,

though you might be rather bored and muddy by the time you arrive. Not all of the towpath is open to cyclists, anyway (check on the British Waterways website www.water-scape.com, which also has information about cycle permits – you may need these to cycle some stretches of towpath outside London, though not in London itself).

Alternatively, you can turn left at Bulls Bridge and scoot down one of England's most enjoyable little stretches of lockside canal downhill, not far from Brentford *(see Caen Hill item on page 30)*. It's about 8km from Southall to Brentford, which has some upmarket restaurants where the Grand Union joins the Thames. You can get a train from here back to central London (Waterloo).

All this plus two tunnels, the Dome, an airport, and a hemisphere crossing

■ Other places like this

It's pretty rare for a canal to cross over a main road. The Shropshire Union Canal goes over the A5 in Brewood, on a tiny aqueduct built by Thomas Telford in 1832, but the towpath looks uncyclable. In Bradwell, Milton Keynes, there's a rather soulless but impressive aqueduct on the Grand Union again, this time over a short stretch of dual carriageway – but at least you can cycle it (OS 152, grid ref SP829411). Built in 1991, this was the first canal system constructed in this country for a century. This also makes it one of the most historic structures in Milton Keynes. And no, you're not too far from the concrete cows. On the Stratford-upon-Avon Canal, about half way between Stratford and Henley-in-Arden, there's a splendidly scary cast-iron-trough aqueduct (a bit like Pontcysyllte's, complete with rail-less drop down one side) that leapfrogs over both a railway and a minor road. Called variously Edstone Aqueduct or Bearley Aqueduct, it's 146m long, the longest aqueduct in England. It's just south of the village of Wotton Wawen (which has another cast-iron-trough aqueduct, vaulting over the A34). The canal has a physically cyclable towpath, but British Waterways don't allow cycling here or almost anywhere else on this particular canal. You can walk it though.

Snackstop

Hungry? If you can stave off hunger until Southall, you're spoilt for choice for genuine, reasonably priced, delicious Indian restaurants with regional cuisine. Our favourite is the Hyderabad, just south of Southall station, next to a tyre place. Lovely Andhra Pradeshi food.

Bevvy break

The Pleasure Boat, Alperton *Rather run-down pub a couple of kilometres past the aqueduct with average beers, but it has a canalside garden.*

Quirkshop

A kilometre or so out of Paddington, on the opposite side of the canal is a large mural made by local schoolkids and artist Kevin Herlihy, pictured at the beginning of this chapter.

Tourer's tick list

✓ Little Venice
✓ Subcontinental Southall

OS 176, grid ref TQ193836
INFO Paddington station information desk, though they may not have a clue about the canal

LONDON UNDERGROUND

WHERE *London: King's Cross Station to Paddington Station (6km one way)*

WHAT *Canal towpath with Underground alternative*

WHY *Car-free London delight, and take your bike on the Tube back*

HOW *Train to either station*

This short flat, almost all car-free, canal ride shows off some of north London's most beautiful (and shabbiest) bits, from Regents Park to station wastelands. It also offers you the odd experience of taking your bike on the London Underground: a little-known option that you are allowed to do in certain circumstances.

North London sights, and take your bike on the tube

Start from Kings Cross/St Pancras (the two stations are adjacent, and Euston is only a few hundred metres away). Leave from the east exit and cycle a couple of hundred metres north up dull York Road. At the lights, go down and left to join the towpath of Regents Canal (steps). From here it's a lovely smooth ride to Paddington through a wide range of north London scenes. You go through Camden Market and then (just after a floating Chinese restaurant on your left) you skirt Regents Park, going right past the zoo's aviary. After that you see some fabulous millionaire homes fronting the opposite bank of the canal. Near Paddington there's a tunnel without a towpath, so you have to come off for a couple of hundred metres – follow your nose – before picking up the canal at Little Venice on a quiet road alongside it. At the basin turn left and follow the canal path for Paddington.

You can return to Kings Cross an unusual way: by tube. You are allowed to take bikes free on a small part of the Underground network at certain times: specifically, 'cut-and-cover' or overground sections, outside rush hour (defined as weekdays 7.30am-9.30am and 4pm-7pm). Essentially that means you can take bikes on some suburban stretches, and the Circle Line. A detailed map is on www.tfl.gov.uk (search for 'tube cycle map'). The Circle Line is the most interesting, because although it's cut-and-cover (ie 'near-surface') it feels properly sub-

terranean. You can't take your bike on the escalators, so you'll have to carry it up down a few (but not too many) steps.

And, standing with your bike inside a tube train carriage, you can enjoy being the target of that very British look: suspicion that what you're doing is not allowed, combined with a reluctance to say anything because it might cause a scene. Staff will be helpful and positive, though (so long as you're in the right place at the right time.)

The tube option is of limited value to most London cyclists: two wheels is almost invariably the fastest, cheapest, safest and most convenient way of getting anywhere within the capital. But the underground alternative can be useful in some circumstances. Cycling visitors unused to hectic London traffic, or those on two wheels just passing through, can for instance take the

park. Cycle paths trace a figure-of-eight on it, enabling you to picnic opposite the Albert Hall; drop into the Serpentine Gallery; skirt the Serpentine; dodge the cool youth showing off their skating moves; have an ice cream by the water's edge; and walk around that daft concrete water-doughnut thing looking for the Diana Memorial, before you realise that it is the Diana Memorial. Hyde Park is a short hop from Buckingham Palace, the Houses of Parliament, and Trafalgar Square.

Circle Line between Euston, Kings Cross/St Pancras, Paddington, Victoria, Embankment (which is directly over the river from Waterloo), Tower Hill (just by the north side of Tower Bridge) and Liverpool Street stations.

At Little Venice, instead of turning left for Paddington, you can turn right and follow another canal –the Paddington Arm of the Grand Union Canal – further *(see page 66)* to Southall, Brentford, or even Birmingham.

If you suffer a mechanical cataclysm, the tube might be a handy way to convey you and machine back home, or to a bike shop, without having to stop and fix it on a dark rainy North Circular. And if you're flying from Heathrow on a cycle holiday,

some of London's most beautiful (and shabbiest) bits

From Kings Cross, you can head east along more of the Regents Canal towpath. However, you'll have to come off the towpath almost immediately and go through Islington on back roads because of a long tunnel. The signage isn't too obvious, but once

you can take the tube virtually all the way across London – so long as the non-peak timings work for your particular departure.

back on the towpath, just after Islington, you can keep heading along the towpath 8km or so down to Limehouse Basin. Tower Bridge, where you can also join the Circle Line to return to your starting point, is along more canal towpath and under 3km away *(see page 58)*. It's a lovely run, but watch for some precariously narrow and steep bits underneath lockside

■ Also in the area...

At Paddington you're close to the north side of Hyde Park, so you could celebrate with a tour of the

bridges. If you turn left just after Victoria Park you still end up at Limehouse, but on a longer loop (around 4km longer) via the Lea.

■ Other places like this

The Circle Line is the most likely option that could be useful for cyclists. Other lines that cyclists might be able to use are the District, East London, Hammersmith & City, and Metropolitan. There are also over-ground parts of other lines, out in the suburbs, that you might be able to use. Check the Transport for London website for the exact details and their useful map of tube lines that take bikes. (Specifically, they include Bakerloo Line: Queen's Park–Harrow & Wealdstone; Central Line: White City–West Ruislip or Ealing Broadway, Leyton–Epping, Woodford–Hainault; Jubilee Line: Finchley Road–Stanmore, Canning Town–Stratford; Northern Line:

Edgware–Colindale, Hendon Central– Golders Green, East Finchley–High Barnet or Mill Hill East; Piccadilly Line: Barons Court–Hounslow West or Uxbridge, Oakwood–Cockfosters.)

London is the only place in England where you can take bikes on metropolitan trains. Newcastle's Metro, England's other such large train system, does not take bikes. (Except folders, of course; but you can take folders everywhere.) Nor do the tram systems in Manchester, Blackpool, Nottingham, Sheffield or Croydon.

You can take your bike in some London black-cabs. For London cyclists this is a useful if pricey way to get your bike home in extreme situations, such as a hopelessly buckled wheel, a broken frame, or an unexpectedly con-vivial dinner party.

London's Floating Towpath

FLOATING TOWPATH

WHERE *London: Tower Bridge circular ride (16km round trip)*

WHAT *Canal towpaths*

WHY *London's backyard, and a unique floating towpath*

HOW *Train to London Bridge station*

This is a traffic- and hassle-free, pleasantly characterful ride round the capital's backyard. It takes in Tower Bridge, a few parks, the 2012 Olympic regeneration area, some East End pub-and-grubs – and a unique floating towpath.

A canal curiosity, through the capital's fascinating backyard

The first bit of the ride, from Tower Bridge to Limehouse Basin, is the same as the 'Lombard St' entry on page 58, but at Limehouse Basin, turn left into the basin itself. Stay on the right hand side and cycle along the towpath to head north-east. It's quite unprepossessing, factory-backyard stuff, but not in any way unpleasant.

The floating towpath is about 2km from the basin: a set of watertop blocks with steel guardrails that ducks under the A12's gloomy over-pass. There's underfloor lighting under the bridge in an extra-terrestrial shade of green. It's something of a ghost-train experience. Back in daylight, the towpath continues for a short stretch until you rejoin dry land at Bow Creek locks.

Now, don't expect too much excitement. 'Floating towpath' might suggest a cakewalk along bobbing pontoons, a makeshift contraption of precarious buoyancy where one slip turns your bike into a metal canoe. Sadly for adventure fans though, the 242m-long structure – though made up of 60 floating sections – feels as firm and stable as the rest of the towpath that cuts straight through the backyard of London's East End. Towpath users had to cross over the busy A12, whose bridge left no room for a conventional towpath, until 2003, when Britain's first hovering solution was completed.

Just after the floating towpath and over a footbridge, a river and canal meet. Views of the navigation and, alongside it, the river, display all kinds of canal inhabitants such as moorhens, herons, and shopping trolleys. Head up the Lea (also spelt Lee) Navigation for 3km, past an enormous converted tidal mill. It used to be a distillery, churning out cheap addictive rubbish to keep the masses entertained. Now it's television studios where programmes like Big Brother are made, so nothing much has changed. There's a supermarket here if you want to stock up on picnic stuff (perhaps for consumption a little later when you pass Victoria Park) or visit the toilet without having to find a canalside bush. This is Stratford; the 2012 Olympics will be based in the area here and to the north, and you'll see lots of regeneration. Even from month to month the waterside changes as derelict buildings come down and shiny new blocks go up.

A bit further up you have to leave the canal, cross a busy roundabout under a flyover, and then rejoin the towpath. It's not signposted, so you'll have to follow your nose. Further on, the canal forks. You keep left. The house at the lock

it's something of a ghost-train experience

was the old home of GMTV, and their watertop weather forecasts were made from here. (It's now a private house.) A little beyond that, you do a U-turn over to the opposite towpath, just where a large canal joins from the left. This is the Hertford Union, and you want to take it. Head along here for 2km – all of it directly alongside Victoria Park – until it reaches another junction, this time with Regents Canal.

At this junction, turn left. You now cycle 3km back to the Limehouse Basin, through the green oasis of Mile End Park. The park features another award-winning bike feature, and this one is definitely less exciting than it sounds: the Green Bridge. It's very much like a bridge, but with considerably more grass than usual. From Limehouse Basin, retrace your route back to Tower Bridge.

■ Also in the area

At the junction mentioned above where you turn left, you can turn right instead to go along Regents Canal towards Kings Cross, about 6km away *(see page 66)*. It's a very pleasant route, with lots of locks as

well as narrow bridges en-route. About 1500m after that right turn is a road bridge. Directly off to your right is Broadway Market. On a Saturday it will be in full swing with expensive but irresistible gourmet stalls. Some markets sell cakes; others sell cakes. These are definitely cakes.

Near Tower Bridge, just off St. Katharine's Dock, is a bendy bike path that is London's answer to Lombard St, in San Francisco *(see page 58)*.

Limehouse Basin is a few hundred metres from Docklands. On a working day this is interesting to explore by bike: a waterside financial district of steel and glass towers, all buzzing with sharp-suited finance workers. You'll be surprised by how many bikes you see parked around the place.

If you don't turn left onto the Hertford Union canal, but stay on the Lea Navigation, you can continue cycling along the canal north for a few dozen kilometres – up through Enfield, and under the M25 towards Hertford (where trains can take you back to London). That would make a good long day trip from the capital.

From Tower Bridge you can cycle all along the Thames (with the odd few metres where you might have to push) east to Greenwich and Woolwich *(see page 62)* or head out west to Slough.

■ Other places like this

London's floating towpath is not quite unique. The scenic and characterful Rochdale Canal (reopened in 2002, running 50km from Manchester to Sowerby Bridge) has recently installed a floatier one south of Rochdale at the point where the canal ducks under the narrow M62 crossing. But this one really is odd – it can be towed out from under the bridge to allow wide boats to pass, though presumably not while you're on it.

The reason for this is that the only route for the canal under the motorway was through a farm-track underpass, which was too narrow to accommodate both a towpath and a wide boat – hence the inventive solution. Last time we looked, though, it still hadn't opened for business. Check the internet for news. The British Waterways' information sheet on towpath cycling says 'refer to local office' for this stretch (Manchester office, 0161 8195847).

Britain has over 6000km of canals, lakes and rivers; for a list of stretches where you're allowed to cycle, go to British Waterways' website at www.waterscape.com. They have a special section on cycling along canals in London. If you want to cycle on a canal outside London, you're supposed to get a permit; you can download one from the website.

Snackstop
House Mill Cafe, Three Mills. *Island Decent coffee, cakes and snacks in a pleasant converted mill a kilometre up the towpath from the floating bit.*

Bevvy break
Bow Bells, Bow Rd. *East End pubs vary, but we had an unpretentious and enjoyable time here, we hazily recall.*

Quirkshop
For traditional East End food, sawdust floor and all, look for the family shop of F Cooke. It's in Broadway, the street with Broadway Market in it (see main text). Here's where you get your actual pie and mash, and jellied eels.

Tourer's tick list
✓ 'Green bridge' in Mile End Park
✓ Broadway Market, just off Hertford Canal
✓ Jellied eels, pie, mash
✓ Tower Bridge
✓ St Katherine's Dock

OS 177, grid ref TQ381821
INFO City Information Centre, St Paul's Churchyard, London EC4M 8BX, tel. 0207 3321456, www.cityoflondon.gov.uk

The Thames Ferries

THAMES FERRIES

WHERE *Central London to Windsor, 60km one way*

WHAT *Thames path, mostly traffic-free*

WHY *Britain's most scenic urban day ride, and a tiny, quirky bike ferry*

HOW *Train to Waterloo (or Putney); return by train*

E
ngland's quirkiest short bike-ferry is across the Thames, near Weybridge. It's the highlight of the mostly car-free riverside day-ride along the Thames Path, which for 60km from the centre of London to Windsor is one of the country's very best full-day cycling trips.

A Thames crossing, and Britain's best riverside trip

You can start in the centre of central London, at the South Bank, and head west along the riverside path. However, the signs will soon take you along quite a few roads. To cut 10km or so of such city riding, take the train from Waterloo to Putney; head north from Putney station to the river and join the riverside path.

All of the Thames Path west of Putney is absolutely gorgeous: car-free, not too muddy, astonishingly rural-feeling, scenic and relaxing. The route passes through Barnes, Chiswick, Kew (where the shrieking of parakeets from the gardens gives the odd impression of cycling under a rainforest canopy), intriguing and delightful Syon House, and then through Richmond and Kingston. At Kingston you cross over the bridge to the north bank for a few kilometres, looping past Hampton Court. The ferry (about 30km from Putney) is just after Walton-on-Thames.

The few kilometres of the Thames Path through and past Walton-on-Thames is lined with houseboats and floating holiday huts. Quarter of an hour after you pass under Walton Bridge, which has the makeshift look of reluctant squaddies' metalwork, you'll see the towpath take a left at a branching-point in the river. The steps down to the ferry – modestly signposted and easy to miss – are immediately on your right, along with a bell and a small sign with information about the boat's running times.

To summon the boat, ring the bell, but only dead on the quarter-hour;

they'll studiously ignore you if you're even a few seconds out. Get it just right, and you'll see the ferry-man appear out of the chandlery shop across the water, walk down to the jetty opposite, and start up his small boat. The ferry has a capacity of perhaps ten or so bikes (though no doubt they'd do a shuttle if there was a large group of you). Seasickness is very unlikely on the 30- second crossing, which at £2 for a person with a bike (£3 return) works out to about the same hourly rate as a rock star's divorce lawyer, but it is all rather fun.

The ferry runs from 8am-6pm every weekday through the year. On Saturdays, it's 9am- 6pm (5pm Oct-Mar); or Sundays, 10am- 6pm (5pm Oct-Mar). If it's closed, cross by Walton Bridge a kilometre or two downriver. It's in two curious parallel sections, the new one for cars and the old one for cyclists.

THAMES VALLEY CYCLE ROUTE

Weybridge ¾
Hampton Court 6
Kingston 10

For all routes use pedestrian & cycle ferry

You're now in Shepperton, whose old centre a kilometre or so up and to the right is another place that looks as if it's been conjured up from postcards. Carrying on upriver though, it's another 15km to Windsor from here. By far the nicest way is to go along to your left alongside the river and past houses beyond description by estate agents (one of which has an amusing Elvis mannequin sitting out on its balcony), but it's one-way the other way; the official path goes along a road until it rejoins the river a couple of kilometres further up.

Carrying on upriver, westwards from the ferry, ride through Staines, and come off the river in Egham, shortly after passing under the M25. From here, go up a hill, past a huge, dignified and silently moving World War II memorial, and into Windsor Great Park *(see page 206)*.

From Windsor, regular trains go back to London. London to Windsor is possible as a day ride, albeit a long one. This is scenery to savour; better budget two days for the trip. Thanks to the easy availability of trains all along the route, you can do it in discontinuous sections.

Gorgeous, car-free, not too muddy, scenic, rural and relaxing

■ Also in the area

In the centre of Windsor is a car-free bridge which takes you over the Thames into Eton, whose main street – with the famous school of course – is interesting to cycle around (it's one-way, south). Windsor is a tourist town in its own right, and small enough to explore on foot if you've had enough cycling. To explore Windsor Great Park though, which you pass through en route, a bike really is necessary. If you're doing the London – Windsor trip in two days, allow a good couple of hours to roam the Great Park and have a picnic. To get the majestic view of The Long Walk, the drive that leads up to Windsor Castle, take a right at the crossroads shortly before the film-set like area of perfect houses and shops called The Village. Unfortunately you can't cycle up the Long Walk.

You can stay overnight in an inexpensive business hotel in Slough, just north of Eton, and cycle from Slough along canals all the way back via Southall to Paddington station, or else to Brentford station.

This part of the Thames Path, ferry and all, is part of National Cycle Route 4, from London to Reading, Bath, Bristol and ultimately St David's in west Wales. After Windsor, Route 4 doesn't stick to the Thames very closely.

From central London, you can cycle east along the Thames out to Dartford, and continue on Sustrans routes to Canterbury or Dover.

■ Other places like this

There are some similar small, bikes-and-people-only ferries right there on the Thames Path, though (unlike the Shepperton Ferry) there's no advantage to using them if you're cycling the riverside. They are Hammertons Ferry ('Ferry to Twickenham' according to the sign on the riverside) and Hampton Ferry, from opposite the Bell Inn, at Hampton.

Interesting ferry-summoning procedures are also available with Felixstowe ferry's table tennis bat and Padstow's Rock ferry, with its yellow flag *(see page 89)*.

At Symonds Yat, in the Forest of Dean not far from Monmouth, we've heard of two interesting ferry experiences. Cyclists can use either of two tiny foot and cycle handworked ferries available all through the day: from the Saracen's Head on the East side, or from the Ferry Inn on the West side. A kilometre or so downriver, along the waterside path, is a thrilling little alternative – Biblins Bridge, a suspension affair with conveniently sloped access. Reedham Ferry – in the Norfolk Broads, not far from Great Yarmouth – is one of the last chain ferries in the country. It's essentially a raft, just big enough for three cars, and provides the only road crossing of the River Yare for a few dozen kilometres between Yarmouth and Norwich. (A curious little swing bridge just downriver carries the railway over it, though.)

Snackstop
Shepperton Lock. *Ideal place for a picnic, with grassy green banks overlooking locks, ferry, and forks in the river. Coin-op toilets by lock, and a tea shop.*

Bevvy break
Thames Court, Shepperton. *Right by Shepperton Lock, a few metres upstream of the ferry on the north side. Riverside garden, pleasant views, decent range of beers.*

Quirkshop
Shepperton Ferry is mentioned in HG Wells's War of the Worlds of 1898, in Chapter 12. This very area, teeming with locals fleeing, is attacked by Martians with their Heat Rays. Nowhere does it say whether the Martians rang the bell to summon the ferry on the quarter hour.

Tourer's tick list
✓ Church Square
  (Shepperton village, 1km
  from ferry)
✓ Hampton Court
✓ Riverside herons, parakeets
  etc
✓ Windsor Great Park

OS 176, grid ref TQ075659
INFO Kingston on Thames Tourist Information Centre, Market Place, tel. 0208 5475592
Tourist.information@rbk.kingston.gov.uk
ferry info tel. 01932 254844

SAVOY COURT

WHERE *London: Tourist circuit (5km-20km)*

WHAT *Picture-postcard sights from the saddle*

WHY *Unlimited photo-opportunities, and a street unique in Britain*

HOW *Train to Waterloo*

This expandable circuit takes you to many of London's best photo-opportunities (Houses of Parliament, Buckingham Palace, Trafalgar Square, the Eye and so on) without the tedium of footslogging – and it also takes you onto the only street in the country where you have to drive on the wrong side of the road. In kilometres it's very short, but will take all day because you'll keep stopping – there's so much to see and do, and photograph.

Cycle on the wrong side of the road, legally

Most of this ride is on roads, but if the traffic feels too hectic at any point, you can get off and push along the pavement.

Start from Waterloo. (Or from Embankment, behind Charing Cross, accessible by tube from anywhere on the Circle Line *(see page 70)*. Head towards the Eye; push your bike along the riverside, or cycle along the backroad, upriver to Westminster Bridge. Cycle across it towards the Houses of Parliament and Westminster Abbey. (The tiny lanes of Westminster College, just south, are fascinating to nose around.) Head west along Birdcage Walk, alongside St James's Park, to Buckingham Palace. Next, head away from the Palace up The Mall (on the car-free path on the left hand side if you prefer). Go under Admiralty Arch into Trafalgar Square. Continue heading straight up the Strand. Just before Waterloo Bridge, on your right, you'll see hoardings for the Savoy Theatre.

Here you can have your unique drive-on-right experience; a little bit of the Continent. As any pub quizzer will try to tell you, the lane on your right is the only place in Britain where you use the right hand side of the road in both directions. The laterally dysfunctional street in question, Savoy Court, is the short in-and-out that leads only to the entrance of the Savoy Theatre and Hotel. For over a century, vehicles have entered and departed on the right-hand side of the road. It's so they can drop off their passen-

gers directly outside the theatre door – which is on the right hand side as you enter Savoy Court – proceed to the front of the hotel, pick up the next fare, turn round, and leave. Driving on the left would mean having to go in and out twice. In 1929, it's said, a special Act of Parliament enshrined this anomaly in law. Strictly speaking it's a private road, and not a public thoroughfare, so does not contravene British traffic regulations – nevertheless, the traffic lights at the junction of Savoy Court and the Strand are indeed on the right, i.e. 'wrong', side, and it's shown as a street on all normal maps.

So, turn off the Strand into Savoy Court on the wrong side, go up to the hotel forecourt, turn round, and return also via the wrong side, waiting at the lights at the end, to rejoin the rest of the country's traf-

fic driving on the left. Stop to admire the shiny hotel canopy – evidently modelled on a Rolls-Royce radiator grill.

Return to Waterloo by crossing over Waterloo Bridge which, thanks to its position on the bend of the Thames, gives the best river-crossing views in the capital. Downriver are St Paul's, Canary Wharf, the Gherkin and the Oxo Tower. The upriver view takes in the Houses of Parliament, Big Ben's Clock Tower, and the Eye. Spectacular by day, it's an even more impressive sight at nighttime. Unlike the car drivers, you can easily stop and pull over onto the pavement to enjoy the views and take a snap or two. But remember to get back on the right side of the road.

> *It will take all day because there's so much to see and do*

■ Also in the area

From Waterloo there's plenty more sightseeing to do from the saddle if you have time. Cycling gently along the promenade from the South Bank downriver takes you past the Oxo Tower and Tate Modern. From there, the Millennium ('Wobbly') Bridge goes over to St Paul's; you can wheel a bike across easily but can't cycle. You can however keep cycling along the south bank promenade past the Globe theatre towards Tower Bridge. Upper Ground is a reasonably quiet road option to return to Waterloo, or you can retrace your steps.

From the Strand, instead of turning right over Waterloo Bridge, you can turn left to cycle around Covent Garden. You'll get pleasantly lost and perhaps find your way back to Trafalgar Square.

Heading upriver from Waterloo, you can follow the promenade by bike a few kilometres, past Lambeth Palace towards Vauxhall and the MI6 building, from where you can have views of the upturned coffee table that was Battersea power station.

Confused by the bridges? Try this mnemonic which tells you the order of cyclable, or at least *cycle-push-able, bridges upriver from Tower Bridge: To List So Many Bridges, Walk Hurriedly West, Looking Very Carefully At Bikes Whizzing Past Bloody Horrendous Car Queues. (TOwer, London, SOuthwark, *Millennium, Blackfriars, WAterloo, *HUngerford, WESTminster, Lambeth, Vauxhall, Chelsea, Albert, Battersea, Wandsworth, Putney, *Barnes, Hammersmith, Chiswick, 'Kew'). An easy way to remember the mnemonic is to memorise the order of bridges and work it out from that.

■ Other places like this

Savoy Court is, so far as we can tell, unique in Britain. There are several places where one-way systems happen to throw together two

adjacent lanes of traffic going the 'wrong way' relative to each other – but there is always some sort of physical barrier between them, and as a cyclist you would naturally go to the left-hand edge of the lane to allow traffic to pass on your right. For example, Ambury in Bath, two minutes' bike west of the railway station; or, reportedly, the approach to Worthing railway station. But Savoy Court is the only road with unseparated wrong-way traffic both ways: here you definitely cycle on the righthand edge of the lane, letting traffic pass on your left.

If you like the experience of cycling on the righthand side of the road, then you can do plenty more in countries where this is the rule. This includes all of continental Europe, Scandinavia, Russia and its sphere, the Middle East, the top two-thirds of Africa, China, North America, and almost all of South America. About two-thirds of the world's people, including the residents of Savoy Court, live in right-hand-drive environments. Drive on left is the rule in the UK, Ireland, Malta, Cyprus, India, Pakistan, Bangladesh, Sri Lanka, Thailand, Macau, Hong Kong, Australia, New Zealand, Indonesia, Papua New Guinea, the other third of Africa from South Africa up to Kenya, Suriname, Guyana, much of the Caribbean, and Japan.

Snackstop

River Terrace Cafe, Somerset House *(summer only)*. *Overlooks the Thames. Entry from Waterloo Bridge north side. Fabulous views, and you can take your bike onto the terrace.*

Bevvy break

The Coal Hole, the Strand. *Woody, atmospheric old pub next corner along from Savoy Court – in fact, it used to be part of the Savoy Hotel. Decent range of cask ales. Bike racks on opposite side of road.*

Quirkshop

Cycle round the 25-foot (7.62m) turning circle at the end of Savoy Court. It's said to have defined the famously tight turning circle of a London taxi.

Tourer's tick list

- ✓ The London Eye
- ✓ Houses of Parliament
- ✓ Buckingham Palace, Admiralty Arch, Trafalgar Square
- ✓ Waterloo Bridge views
- ✓ South Bank promenade
- ✓ Oxo Tower, Tate Modern, St Paul's, Globe

OS 176, grid ref TQ306807
INFO City Information Centre, St Paul's Churchyard, London EC4M 8BX, tel. 0207 3321456, www.cityoflondon.gov.uk

Cambridge
rush hour

CAMBRIDGE

WHERE   *Cambridge: Tourist circuit (5km-20km)*

WHAT   *Picture-postcard sights from the saddle*

WHY   *Unlimited photo-opportunities in Britain's top cycling city*

HOW   *Train to Cambridge*

This is more than just a cycle tour of a photogenic tourist town. It's also to experience the nearest thing here to the Netherlands.

England's Number 1 cycle-friendly city

For a cyclist, Cambridge is the equivalent of an Elvis impersonator finding themselves on a planet of Elvis impersonators. The city teems with cyclists; at rush-hour, mightily so. Not the metropolitan archetypes of lycraed young professional, folding-bike business suit and psycho courier; but the whole range of society. Young and old, rich and poor, trundle along on situp-and-beg bikes, with baskets and bells. In Cambridge, a quarter of the residents cycle to work - by far the highest figure in the country - and some city-centre streets see over 1200 cyclists passing per rush hour. It's wrong to explain it away by the fens' plasterboard flatness, student poverty, or the city's preponderance of middle-class writers. They're factors, but the real reason is that - as in the Netherlands - people cycle because they cycle. The town has a self-perpetuating culture of two wheels, and it makes the experience of rush hour very different from other cities.

Bikes rule. They fill the side streets and flow along the parks. Office workers on their ten-minute commute; rucksack-toting post-doctoral students heading to biotech research centres out west; shoppers whose baskets hold a ciabatta and a bottle of Merlot; undergraduates avoiding lectures.

For the best Cambridge cycling experience, start early (8am or so). From the train station, turn right and cycle through the car park and under the bridge, and keep going in a straight line 2km or so until you hit the river. On weekday mornings in term time (roughly Oct-Nov; mid Jan-mid Mar; mid Apr-mid Jun) students are rowing boats back to boathouses after a morning's training. Coaches on bikes bawl at them from the crowds of cyclists. Carry on upriver along the waterside a few hundred metres. The big green criss-crossed by smooth, straight, well-plied cycle paths is Midsummer Common. There's a good view from the cycle-footbridge.

Follow the cyclists. They will head to another large green, Parker's Piece. More long straight cycle paths traverse this one. They meet in the middle at a single lamppost, whose student name, Reality Checkpoint, has gradually become official. Explore the collegey back streets; there's no obvious single place to observe pedal traffic maxi-

ma, but promising situations might be changeover time between morning lectures (on the hour) at places such as Pembroke St, Trinity St, or Tennis Court Rd.

Clattering down King's Parade, in front of King's College, you'll see the blue bikes of the University Messenger Service, an internal post system for college business. The UMS may not be quite as zippy as email, but they carry fewer bogus offers of cheap pharmaceuticals, anatomical expansion, or riches from third-world banking sleight-of-hand. A UMS message might be a handwritten reference to a recent science journal, sent from the 'prof' you met in the pub last night, that demonstrates the folly of your veiws of the Higgs boson. There's an interesting postbox at King's, too.

Head up and left, crossing the river on the car-free bridge via Garrett Hostel Lane. This much-punted stretch of river is the Backs. You carry on west to a glistening new-tech business park. Microsoft is here, with a vast, tent-topped cycle shed for its employees; when Apple comes to Cambridge, theirs will no doubt be more stylish and easier to use. In this park, the world's finest scientific minds work on new feats of nanotechnology, like designing London cycle lanes. Now, back to the centre with you. It's time for tea and toast, and an Oxbridge-style discussion of Blake and nanotechnology and the Taj Mahal and Caravaggio and Milton Ales and Sibelius and the state of English rugby and damned politicians and the Higgs boson.

■ Also in the area

The world's longest heated, covered, cycle bridge over a railway is right here in Cambridge. In fact, Carter Bridge is the world's only heated, covered cycle bridge over a railway. Just to the north of the station, it provides a convenient hop for walkers and cyclists over the vast outback of railway sidings. Well worth a trundle across. You could easily spend a week cycling round the city and not get bored. Just as well. Topography is not Cambridgeshire's strong point. Heading north-east out of town along the river is nice though, especially in summer.

South, beyond Addenbrooke's hospital, you can cycle along the multicoloured giant bar-code of gene BRCA2 *(see page 169)*.

The many-pubbed village of Grantchester, about 3km along a car-free path on the west side of the river south from the centre, makes an easy and pleasant lunchtime ride.

Cambridge council's useful cycle map, which is on the internet at www.camcycle.org.uk/resources/map, has suggestions of ways to potter outside the city. National Cycle

> *A quarter of the residents cycle to work*

Route 11 (Harlow to King's Lynn) goes through Cambridge.

Cambridge Cycling Campaign is probably the country's most active and effective local body outside London. Their ground-breaking website has route finding software for local cyclists and countless photos, and they put every issue of their excellent magazine online.

■ Other places like this

Various places in England style themselves as 'cycling cities'. Many new towns in the south, like Stevenage or especially Milton Keynes, were built with networks of wide, separated cycle lanes. They often have a soulless feel though; you don't get Beijing-style swarm mathematics, nor the sociable Cambridge bustle.

York's good, perhaps the nearest to a 'northern Cambridge' – lots of cyclists, sometimes decently provided for, a lively student population, calm atmosphere, grand old buildings and a scenic riverside. A day or a weekend cycling around York reinforces the idea that bikes are a valid mode of transport.

Cambridge's academic rival Oxford isn't as much of a bike city, but also has a big cycling rush hour during term time. Broad St is the place to see it.

London has seen a sharp increase in bike commuting over the last few years. Rush hour round the main-line stations, on the bridges, or at places such as Wellington Arch *(see page 54)* are thick with crowds of cyclists. A feature of London commuting is the range of bikes – you see a lot of foldering bikes, especially the ubiquitous Brompton, pedalled by people in suits who come in on suburban trains.

However, the best English towns to find Netherlands-style cycling are Harwich and Hull, because you can take ferries to the Netherlands.

Snackstop

CB2 Bistro, Norfolk St. *Internet access, works from local artists, sells books, live music, good coffee, classy food, and it's a favourite of Cam's cycling movers and shakers.*

Bevvy break

Kingston Arms, Kingston St, Cambridge Off Mill Road. *a pub for good intelligent Cambridge-style conversation, with lots of woody little booths, classy food and fine beer.*

Quirkshop

In the film Chariots of Fire, future Olympic champ Harold Abrahams runs 350m round Trinity College quad in 43 seconds, as the clock strikes 12. It would need world record pace; Abrahams never actually tried it; the scene was filmed elsewhere – but there's nothing to stop you trying.

Tourer's tick list

✓ Kings chapel, colleges
✓ Watch boats on river
✓ Punt up the Backs
✓ Riverside cycle path
✓ Grantchester

OS 154, grid ref TL451587
INFO Cambridge Cycling Campaign, http://www.camcycle.org.uk

RUTLAND WATER

WHERE *Oakham, Rutland: Circular tour of Rutland Water (50km)*

WHAT *Gentle car-free lakeside track*

WHY *Circumnavigate England's largest reservoir and newest lake*

HOW *Train to Oakham*

This gentle, car-free day ride could be the UK's most overlooked biking gem. The circuit of Rutland Water – Britain's biggest reservoir in its smallest county – offers gorgeous villages, period-piece towns, and beautiful waterside family cycling, all in an easy day.

Ride around England's biggest and newest watery secret

Start at Oakham station (about 90 minutes from King's Cross). It has a comfy old-building, English-market-town feel, with a decent complement of pubs, cafes and real shops (but no cycle hire). Trundle round here after breakfast, then head out east along the A606 (a mile or so of main road). You'll soon see on your right, at a junction, the small bike-route signs that indicate the Rutland Water circuit.

'Rutland Water' sounds as if, Lake-District-like, it's been around since the Stone Age. In fact, Britain's most extensive reservoir was still farmland when Abba were in the charts. In 1977, to supply thirsty Peterborough and the East Midlands, the massive man-made lake had its 3,000 acres of blue spilt out onto the countryside just east of Oakham.

Barely an hour's cycle across in any direction, England's tiniest county was known mainly as joke fodder until being abolished in 1974 (as in Eric Idle's TV series Rutland Weekend Television, and Beatles spoof The Rutles, which often mentions Rutland). Through popular demand it was reinstated in 1997, and its motto – multum in parvo, 'a lot in a little' – is apt. And scenic Rutland Water, as big as Lake Windermere, is a curiously over-looked cycling gem. A smooth circular shoreline cycling track, almost all off-road, runs 28km or so around it, with an extra 11km option skirting the peninsula in the middle. It has a fair few slopes, but none

longer than a few dozen metres, and it's excellent for families and mixed-ability (or mixed-motivation) groups. Bring your binoculars and you might even see an osprey.

Most of the time the path is within a stone's throw of the lake. The surface (some tarmac, mostly hard-pack) is all-weather, though if it's throwing it down with rain there are few opportunities to shelter away from the places mentioned above. Conversely, in strong sunshine you'll need hats and sunblock: there are several stretches of shady wood, but none that are very long.

From Hambleton, do a lovely (clockwise) seven-mile circuit of the Hambleton peninsula, giving you a gradual three-sixty panorama of the reservoir shoreline. You see lots of nannyish, litigation-phobic signs sternly warning you to dismount on "steep" hills and badgering you

(three o'clock) takes you to some more gently rolling, smooth paths past Whitwell (one o'clock, something of a watersports centre, with kayaking, windsurfing, and the Rutland Belle pleasure boat doing its hourly afternoon trips; bike hire) and Barnsdale (twelve o'clock) and then back to Oakham.

about helmets. Some of these mild downhills are skiddy gravel, true; but a greater threat comes from the copious sheep poop, which can easily make its way from tyres to kids' fingers, or directly on to drinking-bottle mouthpieces. Hand- and bottletop-washing is strongly advised for kids and adults. Leaving the peninsula, look for the splendid Jacobean Old Hall at eight o'clock on your left.

Rejoining the Rutland Water circuit, you go past the Bird Watching Centre (open daily at nine o'clock) where you can see ospreys – either with your binoculars, or via the live camera. Manton (eight o'clock) is a characterful village with pleasant pubs, and a short section of cycle path alongside a main road turns left down the hill back to the shoreline. (Watch out for hawthorn-related punctures in autumn!) More undulating takes you to the remarkable old Normanton church (four o'clock). There is bike hire here.

The straight flat damtop lane

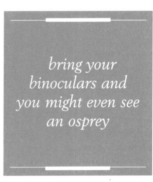

bring your binoculars and you might even see an osprey

■ Also in the area

Eyebrook Reservoir, a few kilometres south south-west of Rutland Water, can be cycled round and is gently scenic – but it's on road and not near a railway station.

Stamford, a perfectly preserved Georgian and early-Victorian town often used as a film location (Middlemarch, Pride and Prejudice, the Da Vinci Code), is a few kilometres to the west. National Cycle Route 63 (Burton-on-Trent to Wisbech via Leicester and Peterborough) takes you from Oakham to Stamford. Perhaps because it lacks a 'killer postcard view', Stamford is less recognisable than say Bath or York. But it's at least as nice to wander round on foot or by bike as they are, has more period-areas to explore, and isn't as self-consciously twee. On a nice evening, take your bikes and a picnic down to the lovely little park on the River Welland just west of the bridge.

Around Rutland Water is a lovely area of England, surprisingly rich in

villages whose period buildings, free of any post-Victorian architecture, look like they've come off a Viewes of England Jigsawe Puzzle: Empingham, North Luffenham, Lyddington and countless more. Lanes are quiet, scenery consistently pleasant, and there are lots of quirky things to cycle up to and investigate. Such as the 82-arch, three-quarter-mile railway viaduct by Harringworth village, south of the Water *(pictured on page 91)*. Completed in 1878, it's Britain's longest, and you can't quite work out why something so spectacular is in this down-to-earth landscape.

■ Other places like this

England has plenty of large lakes and reservoirs that you can cycle round on roads at various distances from the waterside, but none of them have car-free paths right round the shoreline quite like Rutland Water. To circumnavigate Windermere, England's largest lake, involves 40-odd km of main roads, lanes and tracks, not always by the shore (but it's handy for Windermere train station and the Lake District scenery is more eye-catching than Rutland's).

Kielder Water, up in Northumbria, is beautifully set in a wild expanse of forests and hills. It rivals Rutland Water for size (smaller surface area but bigger volume). One side has a minor road and the other a network of forest roads fine for cycling – it's quite a mountain biking centre. It's a very long way from a station though. More accessible is the fabulous circuit round Derwentwater and Ladybower Reservoirs in the Peak District *(see the Mam Tor entry on page 142)*, on very quiet roads or traffic free, easily accessible by rail, and the landscape is superb.

But what makes Rutland Water really odd is its newness: just over thirty years ago you couldn't cycle round it because it didn't exist. In that respect it's hard to find any cycle experience like it.

Snackstop
Harbour Cafe, Whitwell. *Couldn't be handier: right on the water, with tables outside to watch the watersports*

Bevvy break
Horse and Jocky Inn, Manton. *The only pub directly on the lake circuit route. Friendly, decent beer, food, and tables outside*

Quirkshop
Normanton Church, though apparently afloat on the water, in fact sits semi-submerged dry on a bed of concrete. It was scheduled for demolition when the reservoir was built but a campaign saved it. It's now a museum showing the history of the reservoir, worth a visit.

Tourer's tick list
✓ Normanton Church museum
✓ Stamford's time-capsule architecture
✓ Harringworth Viaduct
✓ Quaint villages
✓ Birdwatching
✓ Watersports

OS Landranger 141
INFO Rutland Water Tourist Information, Sykes Lane, EMPINGHAM, Rutland tel. 01572 653026

DEBENHAM

his gently undulating ride through village England is average in every way except the end. The first 19km take you through unremarkable, though not unpleasant, countryside on quiet lanes; tea-shop and pub country, the generic sort of stuff programmed by rota for a cycling club Sunday ride, but the last kilometre is something very remarkable:

Aquaplane on top of a stream on England's longest ford

The longest cyclable ford in the country, which trickles along a lane out of the north-west corner of the village of Debenham.

Start from Stowmarket station and head east through Stowupland, Saxham St, Middlewood Green and Mickfield, villages which punctuate farmland webbed by tracks, back-lanes and the odd fast road. You enter Debenham from the south and cycle up its attractive main street to the north end of the village. The lane you want is The Butts, which runs off to the left. (On OS Explorer 211 it's marked as 'Stony Lane'.) Don't confuse it with another smaller, part-time ford, signposted immediately off the eastern side of the main street; that one will probably be dry anyway.

Britain abounds in this peculiar type of shallow ford. Well, we say ford; it actually stretches the definition to great lengths – lengths such as 100m or more. Unlike a conventional ford, it's not a lateral crossing of a watercourse. It's an uneasy jobshare between road and stream, with small fish temporarily accompanying you on your journey. It's shallow all the way, so the worst that can happen is that you get wet feet, and perhaps turn your bike unintentionally into a site of special scientific interest, thanks to the accumulated pondweed. But on a warm day it's great fun, and most of these long-shallow-fords are either banned to cars or useless to them, so you'll have the water-skimming experience to yourself.

The Butts starts as an innocuous lane heading out of the village, but after a couple of hundred metres it ducks off to the right of a private house. From here the road serves as the stream bed, and the next kilometre is a surprisingly relaxing ride along a mostly smoothish surface, covered by a steady few centimetres of water. There's not a lot to do at the other end, when the stream eventually goes its own way. You could carry on along tracks to rejoin minor roads of your choice, though you may well prefer to reengage with England's longest puddle and head back to the village. There you might enjoy a beer or two at one of the three pubs, and a Sunday lunch. Especially if it's a weekday.

You can return to Stowmarket by any number of back-lane options, though the one that involves least contact with the fast and unpleasant A140 is the way you came. If you're visiting near to Christmas,

then go through Stowupland on the loop through the back of the village rather than the main road. You could see one of the most extravagant light displays in the land.

Stowmarket is on the main Norwich-London line, and the town has the usual sort of services to fill in time or stomachs before your train home.

reengage with England's longest puddle

lots of train options. (One Railway even offers a bike rescue service in Suffolk!) The Suffolk Coastal Cycle Route is National Cycle Route 42, a 75-mile circular route from Felixstowe north to Dunwich and Snape. Sustrans National Cycle Route 1 passes through Beccles and Halesworth before cutting across to the coast on its way down to Felixstowe and Harwich. There are foot and cycle ferries between Harwich, Felixstowe and Shotley and across the Deben Estuary from Felixstowe Ferry to Bawdsey *(see page 99)*. Further north there is a footbridge (you can wheel your bike) and a foot ferry over the Blyth between Walberswick and Southwold.

About 20km east-south-east of Stowmarket is Lavenham, a lovely and relatively unheralded small town of postcard prettiness. It's another excellent base for an easy few days' cycle touring to places such as Sudbury (the nearest train station to Lavenham), Clare, or any of the villages round about.

Sustrans National Cycle Route 51 (Harwich to Cambridge to Oxford) passes through Stowmarket.

■ Also in the area...

The Suffolk area generally is good for easy pottering on a bike, with the next village teashop or pub never far away, and modestly picturesque little villages everywhere.

The atmospheric coast area, which has plenty of excellent bike routes, is a bit of a hike east: Aldeburgh is about 35km away from Debenham, but can be the base of a good long weekend tour, with

■ Other places like this

Rivals to Debenham include Longwater Ford (OS 182, grid ref ST505463), between Wookey and Knowle Moor in Somerset: a likely candidate for the longest ford on a classified road, navigating the River Axe for 100 shallow metres. In Furneux Pelham (OS 167, grid ref TL436280), a horsey Hertfordshire area of wooden-sided thatched houses and quiet rural lanes with mystery Z-bends, is another monster ford: Violets Lane, running north-south. It's usually a farm track of chocolate-sauce puddles *(pictured left)*. But in heavy rain, because it's a couple of metres lower than the fields on either side, it turns into a kilometre-plus, thigh-deep bourn, cyclable only on MTBs by lunatics with snorkels: occasionally England's longest.

Another long aquaplaning-style ford, similar to Debenham's, is at Chobham, Surrey (OS 176, grid ref SU966619): Watery Lane, 100m long *(pictured on page 95)*. With a footpath all the way alongside, you won't be stranded.

Find some more fords near where you are, on the excellent website www.wetroads.co.uk. Among others it lists these – we've arranged them in rough order of suitability for cyclists: Bilbrook, Somerset (OS 181, grid ref ST032412, 66m); Ide, West of Exeter in Devon (OS 192, grid ref SX900906, 100m); Payhembury, Devon (95m); Little Baddow, Essex (45m); Blockley, Gloucestershire (70m); Droxford, Hampshire (183m); East Worldham, Hampshire (700m); Noyna, Lancashire (700m); Lowdales, North Yorkshire (300m); Ruswarp, North Yorkshire (300m); Boggle Hole, North Yorkshire (100m); Bonson, Somerset (200m); Poleshill, Somerset (110m); Great Moor, Staffordshire (300m).

Snackstop
Carters Teapot Pottery, Low Rd, Debenham. *See collectable and novelty teapots being made, then enjoy tea or coffee poured out from one in their cafe.*

Bevvy break
The Woolpack, High St, Debenham. *Friendly, no-nonsense, cosy local pub.*

Quirkshop
Well-respected disc jockey John Peel (John Ravenscroft) lived in the village of Great Finborough, just south-west of Stowmarket, in a thatched cottage called 'Peel Acres'. He is buried in the churchyard there.

Tourer's tick list
✓ Debenham High St houses
✓ Suffolk coast, Aldeburgh
✓ Lavenham

OS 156, grid ref TM166635
INFO Stowmarket Tourist Information, Wilkes Way, Stowmarket, Suffolk IP14 1DE, tel. 01449 916691

Harwich

HARWICH FOOT FERRY

WHERE   *Harwich, Essex, to Saxmundham, Suffolk (40km one way)*

WHAT   *Coastal ride on quiet roads*

WHY   *Scenery, and three remarkable car-free ferries*

HOW   *Train to Harwich, train back from Saxmundham*

This longish, flat day trip follows Regional Cycle Route 41. It gives you atmospheric, very English, coastal scenery – and three remarkable ferries. Too small for cars – in fact, one claims to be the smallest ferry in Europe – they only run in summer, which is in any case the best time to enjoy the big skies and shores of the Suffolk coast.

Curious coastline, and three unique cycle ferries

From Harwich station it's only a kilometre north-west to ferry no. 1: Harwich foot ferry. Board it direct from the shingle beach, up its precarious ramp. The vessel itself is lifeboat-size, and you cram your bike where you can. The two kilometres of crossing takes about ten minutes, and this is one of those experiences that is most atmospheric in spirited weather with three-dimensional seas. It takes you across the harbour mouth's churning waters to Felixstowe (cars doing the same route have a forty-odd kilometre round trip). The fare for a one way trip is £5 (0791 991 1440, www.harwichharbourferry.com).

Vast seagoing vessels, oblivious to you like elephants ignoring birds at a waterhole, throw out wakes to make the water like a roller coaster. You see sprawling concrete scrubland of crates and containers and bustle. Even in midsummer, it can feel like February; everything may be damp and diffuse, but it's a colourful experience.

Disembarking on the other side, follow your nose through the scruffy metal fences and nettles, and hug the coast north through Felixstowe (which is effectively Ipswich-by-Sea). After a few kilometres the town suddenly runs out and you're in the middle of a golf course; shortly afterwards the road stops at a little hamlet, Felixstowe Ferry (it's about 7km-8km from Harwich). Linger here for lunch by the waterside, which is surprisingly active for such a small place. With a popula-

tion of less than 50, the hamlet nevertheless has a boatyard, two pubs, a cafe, those mysterious Martello Towers – and ferry no. 2, Bawdsey Ferry. This one is even smaller, and you summon it by walking to the end of the jetty and waving a table-tennis bat affair with WAVE BAT FOR FERRY written on it. A crossing with bike over to Bawdsey costs £2.50 (summer weekends only, info 07709 411511). The little boat takes you across the mouth of the Deben, which is subject to some surprisingly lively currents.

From here you follow Route 41 signs through quiet, unassuming, very gently rolling countryside. You're on road but traffic is light, as this area's something of a dead end for cars. After about 12km-13km you get to ferry no. 3, which is tinier still: Butley Ferry, claimed to be the smallest licensed ferry in Europe. Volunteers take pedestrians and cyclists in a plastic rowing dinghy across the Butley River. It's only a stone's throw across, but it saves a 7km detour to get to Orford. It costs £1 (summer weekends only, info 01394 450843).

Now you're in the Suffolk coast round Orford and Aldeburgh. It's an

area of Outstanding Natural Beauty, of mammoth skyscapes sketched in watercolours, and vast banks of shingle that make rivers trace bizarre routes. This is also Britten country: England's greatest 20th-century composer lived and worked around here. Much of his music perfectly reflects the look and feel of the landscape. Take the brilliant Peter Grimes for example – ideal sounds for your iPod to accompany a stormy, cold, grey, miserable, heartless, cruel March night.

The Route passes Snape Maltings, a collection of Victorian water-side buildings with shops and venue for regular concerts, to Snape itself, a lovely village. From here it's about 5km north to Saxmundham train station.

mammoth skyscapes sketched in watercolours, and vast banks of shingle

■ Also in the area..

The ferry from Harwich also runs across to Shotley Gate, on the peninsula between the Stour and Orwell. It's quite decent cycling round here, and you might want to do a circuit of Alton Water.

Harwich is at one end point of the Sustrans Hull to Harwich route (which is much nicer than its humdrum-sounding termini suggest), and part of National Cycle Route 1, which runs from Dover to John O'Groats and even the Shetlands.

Harwich is also your gateway to the continent. From here, ferries shuttle you and your wheels over to the Hook of Holland (for the Netherlands' coastal delight of the LF1 Nordzee Route: a relaxed traffic-free, smooth, flat delight for weekenders and families, very highly recommended). You can also get to Esbjerg in Denmark, or Cuxhaven in Germany. If you have several months to spare, Harwich is one of the nodes for the North Sea Route (of which the LF1 is part). It's a mammoth 6,000km long circuit of the waters. Clockwise starting from Harwich, it goes up the eastern side of Britain, traverses Orkney and Shetland, and links to Bergen in Norway via ferry. From there you can follow the coast through Sweden, take another ferry across to Denmark, go round the Jutland peninsula, and follow the coasts of northern Germany

and Holland, before finally taking the ferry from the Hook of Holland back to Harwich.

■ Other places like this

The boat from Rock to Padstow, across the mouth of the Camel estuary in Cornwall, is – like Felixstowe's – a ped-and-bikes ferry that you summon in an interesting way, in this case by waving a yellow flag. If you've just spent all morning cycling across Cornwall's hilly countryside you may feel a white one more appropriate. The ferry runs all year.

Once across in the bustling harbour of Padstow, you can enjoy an overpriced fish speciality at one of its restaurants. Or, perhaps, enjoy the free Camel Trail *(pictured on page 99)*, a picturesque rail trail along the estuary, right out from Padstow, that's one of England's showpiece leisure-cycle routes. The flat, traffic-free route takes you 10km to Wadebridge; a mar-

ginally more adventurous 14km continues to Bodmin, and there are plenty of bike hire opportunities along the way.

Vehicle ferries over estuaries include the free Thames ferry at Woolwich *(see page 62)*, and Mersey's historic and sociable shuttle *(see page 154)*. Car-free ferries include the seven-minute crossing from Portsmouth railway station to Gosport (said to be England's biggest town without a train station) for £2.70 return (www.gosportferry.co.uk). And in Devon, an hourly summer foot ferry operates from Exmouth to Starcross (which has a rail station on the dramatic waterside stretch of the line to Penzance) across the mouth of the Exe. It's a fiver one way including bikes.

Snackstop
Ferry Cafe, Felixstowe Ferry. *Smashing little cafe right by the tiny ferry to Bawdsey; sit outside and watch the ferry.*

Bevvy break
Ferry Boat Inn, Felixstowe Ferry. *Charming old pub near the ferry where you can sit outside on a verandah.*

Quirkshop
Snape is on the River Alde, one of Britain's oddest watercourses. It reaches the sea at Aldeburgh – but doesn't enter it. Instead it turns right for 14km, separated from the sea by a narrow bank of shingle, down way past Orford (where it is now the River Ore) before hitting the sea only a few kilometres north of Bawdsey Ferry.

Tourer's tick list
✓ Fresh seafood from hut in Old Felixstowe
✓ Picnic by waterside watching boats and ships
✓ Big-sky Suffolk coast
✓ Snape maltings
✓ Harwich for the continent

OS S169 grid ref TM258328
INFO Tel. 0791 991 1440, www.harwichharbourferry.com

THE DUNWICH DYNAMO

DUNWICH DYNAMO

WHERE *Hackney, north London, to Dunwich, Suffolk (200km one way)*

WHAT *Annual midsummer through-the-night mass bike ride to the coast at dawn*

WHY *Growing cult event with amazing buzz; do it before it gets mainstream*

HOW *Meet at pub in Hackney, coach back from Dunwich*

They say it started in 1993 when a few London couriers went for a long ride one summer evening, and stopped when their feet got wet. Now it's one of the big cult events in the London cycling calendar: over 700 people riding 200km through the night from a London pub to see sunrise at the coast in Dunwich about 9-10 hours later.

The bike equivalent of the London Marathon

It's not for charity, it's not organised, it's not a race. It's not a demo or a commemoration, it has no official start or finish line, and there are no medals or certificates for those who complete it. In fact, it's not for anything, it's just a very long ride in the dark with a lot of people; the biggest peloton, perhaps the biggest cycling buzz, you'll ever be part of. It's gloriously pointless, often rather painful, and it's done just for sheer collective enjoyment, like football or opera. Or life.

Soon its growing media coverage will make it mainstream, and it'll get all corporate and sponsored, and involve reality TV celebs and people in carrot costumes. So do it now while it's still cool. The ride is in late July each year; 2008's is on Saturday 19 July, starting roughly 8.30pm at the Pub on the Park, Martello St. Details are on the web at www.southwarkcyclists.org.uk.

Here's the diary of our special correspondent N, who did the ride in 2006.

8pm I'm amazed to see 400 cyclists milling around on the corner of London Fields nearest the pub. Expectation in the air. A4 sheets are on sale for £1 giving details of the route.

8.30pm Suddenly, people start to depart and we join them. The first few kilometres, through Hackney's back streets and lanes, cause some local surprise.

9.30pm Out of the street lights here. The riders have settled out into single file, still only a few metres apart. The overwhelming image is of a long line of red LED rear lights stretching into the distance, being overtaken by a steady stream of rather surprised motorists.

11pm Through Epping Forest, over the M25, and into the small town of Epping: 25km gone, still 175km to go. Local drinkers are generally curious. Past Epping is the most magical section, between here and the half-way point. It's dark now, and the roads are getting rapidly quieter. But we're still high on excitement and haven't begun to get tired. I latch on to a group of faster riders. I'm absolutely loving it at this stage, and all that matters is the name of the next little village on the route sheet, and the distance done so far.

12 midnight Great Dunmow. A few boisterous drunks.

3am Sudbury, just before the halfway stop. Still a few drunks about. The roads are silent except for the hum of tyres on tarmac, and empty

cyclists outside the cafe at Dunwich, and bikes all over the place. A buzz. People are lying down on the beach to sleep. However, I'm feeling fresh as a...

(At this point, the diary becomes illegible and ceases abruptly.)

■ *Also in the area...*

When you arrive at Dunwich's steep shingle beach, it's possible to do some more cycle touring round here – the area is good to explore by bike – but it's unlikely your backside will let you contemplate any more cycling for a few thousand years. Some crazy people turn round and cycle back to London, or head up the coast for a Sunday spin; but the vast majority snooze on the beach. Many people have a wake-up swim on arrival (so take swimming stuff and a change of clothes). The cafe opens specially at 6am; the pub opens at 12 noon.

except for the jamjar night-lights set out every mile or so to mark the way, like the twinkling gangways in aircraft safety demos. Few cyclists in sight.

3.30am The night lights stop at the halfway point, a village hall in Great Waldingfield, where refreshments are miraculously served and woozily consumed.

Dawn gradually takes over and my body notices what is going on. Kilometres 100 to 150 are by far the hardest. This is a slog.

6.30am Past the 150km the new day has definitely started. The proximity of the destination gives me a certain amount of second wind. But not much.

9am The approach to Dunwich is remarkable: heathland which is quite different from what has gone before. At last comes Dunwich and the coast, with a large gaggle of

the biggest peloton, perhaps the biggest cycling buzz, you'll ever be part of

To get back, the nearest train station is Darsham, four miles from Dunwich – you can book in advance, but bike places will be limited and engineering works often turn Sunday trains into buses, so this isn't a good option. Instead, take the special coach for the snooze home. Southwark Cyclists' website says: "We put the bikes in furniture vans with their professional packers. Tandems and recumbents fit easily.

If you're worried about your pristine paint job then bring a wrapping sheet or blanket or similar but we're asking the firm to bring lots of cardboard etc... The vans load from 11am and leaves Dunwich Beach at 1pm, getting to West Smithfield, London EC1 (Smithfield Market) about 2 hours later". Tickets are about £14 and can be booked over the internet at www.southwarkcyclists.org.uk – early booking advised.

■ Other things like this

There are any number of mass distance charity rides in Britain, the 90km London-to-Brighton being the most celebrated. This is Europe's largest cycle event, run in June each year, in aid of the British Heart Foundation. For more information, see www.bhf.org.uk. It attracts over 25,000 cyclists. Fundraising is part of the deal.

If it's medium-distance rides (without having to rattle a tin round your friends) that you're after, your local branch of the CTC (the 'Cycle Touring Club', or officially 'Cycle Touring and Campaigning') is the place to look (www. ctc.org.uk).

And if you want extreme long-distance rides with a few fellow riders, contact Audax, the long-distance cyclists' association (www.audax. uk.net). These are the sort of people who would do the Dunwich Dynamo, have breakfast, then turn round and cycle back to London. One ride directly inspired by the Dunwich Dynamo is in Devon: the Exmouth Exodus is a full-moon midsummer 160km night-ride to the seaside (see www.exmouthexodus.co.uk).

Snackstop
Great Waldingfield. *Tea and refreshments at bleary-eyed halfway point, if you're early enough (take some change). Take fuel with you too, especially quick-fix sugar-rush fodder such as chocolate and energy bars, and lots of water!*

Bevvy break
Pub on the Park, Martello St, London Fields, Hackney. *Start point loosely between 8pm and 9pm. The Ship Inn in Dunwich opens at noon...*

Quirkshop
A thousand years ago wool-rich Dunwich almost rivalled London. Coastal erosion means the medieval metropolis is now half a mile offshore, on a quiet night they say you can hear the watery tolling of the lost church bells.

Tourer's tick list
✓ Swim on arrival
✓ Sleep through rest of day
✓ Enjoy bragging rights for rest of year!

OS 176, grid ref TQ 347843. Buy a route leaflet on night in the pub
INFO www.southwarkcyclists.org.uk/dunwichfaqs.htm;
www.rapha.cc/index.php?page=144

Cycling
The Fosse Way

FOSSE WAY

WHERE *Bath, Somerset to Kemble, Gloucestershire (30km one way)*

WHAT *Scenic, quiet mix of quiet roads and car-free paths, most dead straight*

WHY *Historic feel of Roman Road, and odd slice through countryside*

HOW *Train to Bath, train back from Kemble*

This curious, charming, quiet day ride takes you almost in a dead straight line along the Fosse Way, once a major Roman Road stretching over 350km from Exeter to Lincoln.

How Roman cycling would have been. If they'd had bikes

Oxford Street is a Roman Road. The A2 is a Roman Road. That dull, lavishly nettled farm track near you, marked on the OS map by a black dashed line as if inviting you to cut it with scissors, is a Roman Road. There's nothing olde-worlde or charming about a lot of Roman Roads. There's little point in cycling the Fosse Way where it is now the A30, A35, A37, A433, A429 and A46, or even the B4455 and B4114. But the 30km or so that runs northeast from Bath up to about Kemble is something a bit special, and possibly the closest to what cycling for the Romans would have been like. Among pleasant if unspectacular scenery, there's a subtly cumulative oddness about this section. Unlike other country lanes, it doesn't just dawdle from one hamlet to another, swerving round imaginary obstacles en-route like a drunken village idiot. After Bath it avoids habitation altogether, as if you'd cycled into a 1950s B movie where all human settlements have been beamed away by aliens. The chaotic succession of tiny lanes, tracks and byways maintain a more-or-less straight line, as if it had a secret purpose known only to the faithful. (It does: Lincoln.)

From Bath station head along London Road, straight out northeast from the city centre − the old Fosse Way. In Batheaston, fork left just after the George & Dragon and White Lion pubs, and go up Bannerdown Road. Fosse Lane, to its left, is presumably the original

route, but gets lost on top of the hill where the track becomes indistinct. After a couple of kilometres climb it reaches the top of a landscape of sawn-off hilltops, and back on the linear Fosse Way.

From here is a glorious stretch of straightness, often on slender tarmac lanes canopied by trees, with the occasional shimmy to right or left for a valley crossing. After

crossing a main road at a pub called The Shoe, the lane gets narrower. Passing under the M4 at Fosse Gate, the tarmac runs out for a bit. Hold up the OS map nearly flat in front of you at eye level and see how little it deviates. Beyond Easton Grey is a stretch for 12km or so offroad. This is the most atmospheric section, and the one most unchanged from two millennia ago. Typically it's on gravel, a surface similar to what tha Romans would have found familiar. High hedges line either side, as if it were a time tunnel.

The road crosses quaint little old

bridges (such as that near Easton Grey) or across remote fords hardly changed since Roman times, such as the two in succession near Brokenborough; there's always a dry alternative way round. Farmland moves gently up and down as if breathing lightly, and you'll hardly see a soul. Things peter out between Tetbury and Kemble, at an airfield. From here it's all main roads as far as Lincoln Cathedral. Maybe this is a good time to get the train at Kemble station and head back.

High hedges line either side, as if it were a time tunnel

(see K&A Aqueducts on page 18). Bath is on the National Cycle Network Route 4, which goes from London to St David's in west Wales.

Many of the villages just off the Fosse Way are picturesque in a Cotswoldy way and have refreshment. If you don't mind stretches of road cycling, picturesque (but touristy) places such as Bibury or Bourton-on-the-Water are good stops on a touring itinerary. National Cycle Route 45, which goes from Salisbury to Chester, crosses the Fosse Way at Cirencester, a few kilometres beyond Kemble.

There's little point following the Fosse Way beyond Tetbury to Lincoln; it's mostly fast main roads. If you do make it to Lincoln, though, there's another straight Roman Road: Ermine Street Rome's London-to-Lincoln trunk road, going ultimately to York. Explore Lincoln's timeless cobbled lanes, and pause to admire only Roman road arch that you can cycle under in the world (pictured on page 106). From here north to the Humber is classical Roman, dead straight (except for an airfield detour) and switchbacking. The nicest bits are the old lanes, now bypassed, north from Hibaldstow. The Romans ferried the Humber across to Brough and thence York; now there's the Humber Bridge (see page 158) and a Sustrans National Cycle Route.

■ Also in the area...

The train back from Kemble can take you to Bristol Temple Meads, from where you can cycle the country's best rail trail to get back to Bath (see Staple Hill Tunnel on page 22). There are plenty of great cycling opportunities around Bath

■ Other places like this

There are plenty of olde-Roman-Road experiences across England *(see Cam High Road, page 182)*. Here is a selection:

South-east: Stane Street From Epsom, head south south-west from the racecourse along Pebble Lane; the high ground is an old track, just as it was when this was Stane Street, the main route to Chichester. Down at the Chichester end of Stane St (now the A29) there are delightful and smoothish paths in secluded Eartham Wood. Cycle the Stane to Eartham from Bignor, where there's a Roman Villa as well as a crossroads with the ancient (and MTBable) South Downs Way. Fishbourne *(see Bosham Harbour, page 34)* is also nearby.

East Anglia: Cambridge to Haverhill A splendid bridleway running south-east, past a vineyard for that Latinate feel.

East Anglia: Peddar's Way An easy, gently undulating day's ride of wide skies, wildlife and water-colour richness. Try the 30-odd kilometres in North Norfolk (Fring south towards Holme Hale) – mainly green lanes, with the odd stretch along tarmac.

North: Dere Street This road took the Romans from York to Scotland, and is now variously the A59, B6265, A1, B6275, and lots of tracks. At Consett it crosses Sustrans' Coast to Coast route *(see page 178)*, and in Bishop Auckland it's the narrow steep street of Wear Chair. North of Corbridge (museum and Roman Fort) you pass through Hadrian's Wall. North of Rochester in Northumberland things get interesting when Dere St turns right from the A68: offroad though so you'll need mountain bikes.

Snackstop
AV8 Restaurant, Kemble Airfield. *Kemble itself is a bit bare, but the airfield (right on the path of the Fosse) is open to the public, and contains this bistro-restaurant.*

Bevvy break
Shoe Inn, North Wraxall. *Right on the Fosse Way.*

Quirkshop
The source of the River Thames is at Thames Head, a kilometre's walk north-west of the A433 (which is a busy continuation of the Fosse Way) a couple of kilometres due north of Kemble (OS 163, grid ref ST 981993). From the main road there's a grassy footpath (the start of the longdistance footpath the Thames Path) along which you can wheel your bike.

Tourer's tick list
✓ Bath: city, river, canal
✓ Hobnob with royalty in Tetbury

OS 172, grid ref ST780674 to 173, grid ref ST945950
INFO Tetbury Tourist Information, 3 Church St, Tetbury GL8 8JG, tel 01666 503552, tourism@tetbury.org

ASTON CLINTON

WHERE *Tring, Herts to Wendover, Bucks (15km)*

WHAT *Back roads and canal paths in home counties scenery*

WHY *'Freewheel uphill' on country-lane optical illusion*

HOW *Train to Tring, train back from Wendover*

This quiet, varied ride of lanes, canal paths, cottages and hills between two pleasant home counties towns enables you to do a minor cycling miracle: freewheeling uphill. This 'magnetic hill' is on Dancersend Lane, a thread of tarmac round the back of Wendover Woods.

Freewheel uphill in rural Buckinghamshire

Start from Tring station and head west towards Tring. The name suggests bakelite phones, as does the town itself, replete with ideal pub, shop and sausage roll opportunities. There's a cycle path on the pavement virtually all the way. Go right through the town. Don't turn left up the lane signed 'Dancers End' just outside the town – carry on up to the big double roundabout.

a rewarding free scoot is due; yet you're still having to pedal, and soon the road resumes its upward climb. This stretch, between sign and gate, is the gravity bit. Turn round, and stop by the gate: you'll then experience that odd rolling-uphill sensation.

Now don't get too excited, you won't exactly feel yourself battling some miraculous force-field, like a

Follow the signs to Aston Clinton, and on the straight downhill after the double-roundabout, take the first left (signposted Wendover B4009) then immediately first left up the lane (signed 'Dancers End', though the loose, swivelling sign might be pointing anywhere).

The bottom hundred metres of Dancersend Lane is, in itself, mildly disorienting in its gentle slope. Just past Icknield House on the left, you might feel you're going downhill when in fact it's gently up. But carry on for 500m or so, up a long straight climb. The brow of the hill rises, and you eventually crest it – apparently. Between the sign for horse riders on the left, and the gate on the right, it feels as though

cartoon character being pulled towards a fizzing giant horseshoe magnet after some anvil-swallowing mishap. This is not the Roswell Incident, it's only 50m of rural Buckinghamshire. But it is rum, and however many times you do it, your eyes and feet still won't quite agree on what's happening.

All that's going on is that the immediate horizon and field furniture happens to slope in a way that fools the eye. The brain calibrates its zero-gradient from the ground level of the field and the hedge profile, and insists to your feet that the road must be uphill. The quickness of the land deceives the eye. The effect is heightened because this stretch comes between two steeper

different line from Tring. You may find it easier to retrace your steps to Tring and take the train back from where you came.

■ Also in the area...

A 38km section of the Icknield Way – once plied by Boudica and her Iceni in their shin-slicing chariots – has Wendover roughly in the middle and is a good day's mountain biking. Wendover Woods, just by the town, has a number of family cycling trails; here you're sure to see the rare firecrest, Europe's smallest bird, if only because it's pictured on the signs.

sections sloping in the same direction; your mental spirit-level mistakes it for an opposing slope in respite. On a weekend this is a popular spot for local families bring the kids on a Sunday drive.

Return down the hill to the junction at Bucklandwharf and turn left onto the canal path. At Halton village you have to take the road for bit, but rejoining the canal takes you into Wendover *(pictured on page 106)*. Sounding like the set-up to a double entendre

however many times you do it, your eyes and feet still won't quite agree

Not far from Wendover, the recent Phoenix Trail runs from Thame to Princes Risborough – another Sustrans family gem along on old railway, with sculptures and smooth all-weather surfaces. The Grand Union canal runs through Tring, and branches peel off to Wendover and to Aylesbury. The towpaths offer flat offroad alternatives from

in a Two Ronnies sketch, it's actually lovely little market town, with thatchy cottages, shoppes, a High Street that happens to be the Ridgeway, and a delightfully friendly Tourist Information. Chequers, the Prime Minister's country retreat, is just a stone's throw away – an appealing thought for those with a good arm. You can take a train from here, though it's on a completely

both Tring and Wendover to Dancersend Lane.

Cycling all the way from Tring to Bucklandwharf along the Wendover towpath may one day be possible: the canal is gradually being restored and by 2010 (we assume) the path will be cyclable. At the moment though there's a 3km stretch in the middle (where the canal is currently dry) that's foot-

path only, and ankle-deep in mud. What you can do though, for flat car-free rural trundling, is cycle right from Tring station along the Grand Union towpath up to Marsworth, then left along the Aylesbury Arm to Aylesbury – around 13km in total. Sustrans National Cycle Route 6 (Windsor to the Lake District) runs through Luton; NCR30 and 57 run through Wendover.

■ Other places like this

Magnetic hills, gravity hills, however you describe them, there are hundreds of such optical illusions that apparently stick two fingers up to Newton's First Law of Thermodynamics. There are hundreds of examples around the world, and one (in Moncton, Canada) has even been turned from a dusty rural farm track into a tacky theme park.

The best gravity hill in Britain is Scotland's Electric Brae ('Croy Brae') in Ayrshire, on the A719 south of Dunure. It's even marked as such on the OS map. At a few hundred metres long, it is many times longer than any English examples, and even has signs warning motorists to watch out.

England has a handful of magnetic hills, but finding them is an inexact science; maps are no help. It's all subjective, and depends on someone sober noticing the effect and noting it for the later reference of a mapmaker. An article in issue 291 of the Fortean Times, the journal of strange phenomena, cited "a hill near Yetminster in Dorset", and Magnetic Hill on the A3055 between Shankill and Ventnor on the Isle of Wight. Diligent trawls on the internet and should reveal fuzzy references to Bath Road between Lansdown and Tracy Park Golf Course outside Bristol and, more promisingly for cyclists, Hangman's Hill at High Beach in Epping Forest.

Snackstop
Atkins Bakery, Tring. *On main street, has tables outside. Soup, sausage rolls, coffee and other cycling snackery.*

Bevvy break
Red Lion, High St, Wendover. *Grand, half-timbered old coaching inn with outside seating for you and bike, and selection of real ales.*

Quirkshop
The rare firecrest is Europe's smallest bird: only 9cm long, but prominent thanks to its golden colour and black and white go-faster stripes. The Firecrest Trail in Wendover Woodland Park is a footpath, but the park's Cycle Trail joins large parts of it. The firecrest is there all year, in bushes and conifers, making a 'zi-zi-zi-' call.

Tourer's tick list
✓ Canal towpath
✓ Wendover
✓ See a firecrest
✓ Phoenix trail

OS 165, grid ref SP901107
INFO Wendover Tourist Information Centre, The Clock Tower, High St, Wendover, Bucks HP22 6DU, tel. 01296 696759, tourism@wendover-pc.gov.uk

NETHERTON TUNNEL

WHERE *Across Dudley, West Midlands (7km)*

WHAT *Canal towpaths*

WHY *Longest car-free tunnel you can take a bike through in UK*

HOW *Train to Old Hill, train back from Tipton*

It's a little-known fact that if you took all the tourist brochures telling you the area has more miles of canal than Venice and laid them end to end, they would stretch for 51.5km, exactly the length of all the canals in Birmingham. This short towpath ride takes you through a unique, astonishing, and rather scary piece of engineering: Netherton Tunnel, which is nearly 3km long.

Potholing by bike: Britain's longest motor-free tunnel

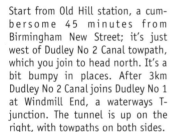

Start from Old Hill station, a cumbersome 45 minutes from Birmingham New Street; it's just west of Dudley No 2 Canal towpath, which you join to head north. It's a bit bumpy in places. After 3km Dudley No 2 Canal joins Dudley No 1 at Windmill End, a waterways T-junction. The tunnel is up on the right, with towpaths on both sides.

Sigmund Freud would have had all sorts to say about Netherton Tunnel. Going through it with a bike is challenging. Not physically, but psychologically. The only point of reference in the 2768m of arrow-straight pitch-darkness is the pin-prick of light in the distance, piercing thinly like Venus in a heartless winter night sky. Victorian narrow-boaters were fearful of ghosts roaming the lonely catacombs: spectral remains of the navvies who had perished during the canals' harsh, dangerous, candlelit construction, maybe. Many avoided the tunnels altogether, and took enormous detours to do so.

You quickly understand why. Here in the gunbarrel acoustic, the merest swish of rainjacket sleeve or drip of condensation from the chill stone walls reverberates on the acoustic mirror of the water surface for ever. When you're deep in mid-tunnel,

1300km from the nearest living soul in either direction, you hear a chorus of whispering spirits, sounds that come out of nowhere but which refuse to die. You are alone with them, whoever - whatever - they are. Make no mistake, this is a weird experience.

The towpath is a bit rough but OK; there's a guardrail all the way which doesn't give you much wobble margin, and the headroom is just enough for a six-footer. The towpath is marked on the OS maps as a footway, and walkers do occasionally use the tunnel. There are no 'No Cycling' signs, presumably because so few people try it, but this length of canal does not appear on British Waterways' list of towpaths where cycling is allowed. So, officially, walk your bike through the tunnel.

If you go through the tunnel with friends, when lots of cheerily-flash-lit walkers and party boats are passing, you may think it weedy to be scared by a piece of civil engineering. But alone it is different. You'll certainly need lights, and maybe a Bible or Qur'an. There is no illumination, save a couple of arrows of daylight from ventilation shafts, and the moon of the entrance waning behind. And it's a long, long, long way through.

The plentiful canalside cycle-touring opportunities in Birmingham would fill a decent book, and they have: Nicky Crowther's very handy Birmingham Cycle Guide. You can also find useful suggestions on the internet (www.waterscape.com).

The Birmingham City Council website (www.birmingham.gov.uk), but does require you to fill in a form and have them post it to you. Follow any old canal path that looks interesting and some reasonably interesting townscapes are bound to present themselves before long. Head south (along Dudley Canal No. 1) or east (along Dudley Canal No. 2, which has a 500m tunnel at Gosty Hill, but since it has no towpath, it isn't traversable) from Netherton Tunnel for example.

From the north end of the tunnel, heading left along the Wolverhampton Level canal for

Out on the other side, the towpath goes immediately under a canal aqueduct, then joins the Main Line Canal at Dudley Port junction. Tipton station is only a couple of kilometres up the towpath left, from where you're only 20 minutes from Birmingham New Street. You're now at the junction of an extensive network of canals with endless towpath options; if you fancy some easy, flat exploration, see the book mentioned later on.

three kilometres or so leads to the Black Country Museum. An urban heritage park, built around a reconstructed canal village, with pub, shops and inland port, the museum offers time-travel activities like riding on trams, visits to a 1920s cinema or going to an old school lesson.

Boat trips are also available through Dudley Tunnel, which is longer than Netherton but doesn't have a towpath. The Birmingham area is well worth a long weekend

> *Victorian narrowboaters were fearful of ghosts roaming the catacombs*

exploring by bike. If your memories of the place are of dreary National Express stopovers, cycle round the spiffy Gas St Basin area to see how the place is rapidly regenerating.

■ Other places like this

Netherton is an anomaly - the only one of the 20 longest canal tunnels with a towpath. Why? Because the others date from pickaxe days; carving out space for a towpath was uneconomic, so you can't get a bike through, except by boat.

The next longest with a towpath is Chirk Tunnel, at 459m, on the Shropshire Union just south of Chirk railway station. The longest canal tunnel where cycling is definitely allowed could be the 433m long Shrewley Tunnel, on the Grand Union just west of Warwick, with a curious elevated towpath.

The longest cyclable traffic-free tunnel on a rail trail that we know of is the 471m one at Staple Hill, *(see page 22)*. Putting traffic-free requirements to one side, the longest tunnel of all that you can cycle through in Britain is the Queensway Tunnel that arcs under the Mersey, between Liverpool and the Wirral. It's a whopping 3237m, but cycling is only allowed at night (that is, not 6am-8pm Mon-Fri, 7am-8pm Sat, nor 8am-9pm Sun, though it is allowed at any time on Sundays from 1 Oct-31 Mar).

The next longest cyclable road tunnel is probably Rotherhithe, under the Thames (1481m). It is open 24/7, but car noise and fumes make neither it nor Queensway offer pleasant cycling experiences.

Snackstop
Picnic. *Bumble Hole, a park area has a visitor centre, toilets and places to picnic. An Aldi supermarket is not far.*

Bevvy break
Little Dry Dock pub, Netherton. *Delightful pub near the southern end of Netherton Tunnel. The bar is made from half an old boat, they do good real ale, and Desperate Dan Cow Pies, complete with horns.*

Quirkshop
The Wikipedia page on the town of Tipton, at the north end of the tunnel, claims that the local dialect is similar to that spoken by Shakespeare or Chaucer. This does not sound convincing given our experiences there of asking directions to the supermarket.

Tourer's tick list
✓ Explore canal network
✓ Have a balti
✓ Black Country Museum

OS 139, grid ref SO 954884
INFO Tourist Information Centre, Churchill Centre, Ednam Rd, Dudley, West Midlands DY1 1HL, tel. 01384 812812

Blackpool Bridge

BLACKPOOL BRIDGE

WHERE *Circular ride from Lydney, Gloucestershire (min 8km round trip, max 40km)*

WHAT *Forest and rail trails, mostly car-free and family-friendly*

WHY *Gorgeous forest cycling, and Britain's only intact Roman Road junction*

HOW *Train to Lydney*

This set of family-friendly, easy, scenic circular trails round the Forest of Dean in Gloucestershire needs little excuse, but a tiny detour takes you to a piece of road history: the only surviving exposed Roman road junction in Britain. In fact, there are arguably only two other significant stretches of original Roman road surface in the country, Wade's Causeway and Blackstone Edge, see below, and this is the one most conveniently visited by bike.

Original Roman Road surface, deep in the Forest of Dean

Start from Lydney train station and cycle north 6km along the B road to Parkend. The scenic Dean Forest Railway runs heritage trains along this route in summer and takes bikes by arrangement - see www.deanforestrailway.co.uk

Parkend is on a system of off-road bike routes, going along old railway lines and forest roads. Follow the trail marked by posts with yellow track marks and starting near the Woodman Inn pub. North 4km from here is the Pedalabikeaway cycle centre, the hub of the bike trail system. Their website has a PDF map of the forest trails the main option, Family Cycle Route, is a circular 20km; www.pedalabikeaway.co.uk. It's pretty flat, which can be important in such a hilly place. Another bike hire centre, PedalAway (www.pedalaway.co.uk), is at Llangarron.

Cycle your way to about five o'clock on the Family Cycle Route and come off near Mallards Pike to join the B4431. Cycle east a few hundred metres until you see a junction with a minor road off to the left (to Soudley), crossed by a disused railway bridge. Just beyond the bridge, running parallel on the left of this shaded, quiet forest lane, is your historic road: the a stretch of rough cobbles that looks like a neglected footpath.

A sign cautiously refers to it as 'An ancient paved road known locally as The Roman Road'. Many sources say that it probably is Roman, despite its being about half the width you'd expect: that's apparently because it's not a via but an actus, a kind of Roman B-road. It would have been a smoother walk back then, with a surface layer of gravel packed across the top of the cobbles. Surviving Roman road surfaces are rare; after they left, around the end of the

fourth century, lesser-used roads fell slowly into overgrown disrepair and paving stones were looted for building, while regularly used routes were repaved over many times. Only in a few remote places have original surfaces remained.

Follow the course of the road north. Just before the stream, where the surviving surface ends, are the remains of a junction - said to be the only surviving Roman example in Britain. The left fork curves off across the stream, via the old Roman ford, and disappears into bramble thickets beyond. The right fork goes under the present road and crosses the stream as 'Blackpool Bridge'. They say all roads lead to Rome; well, this one only goes to Upper Soudley. Perhaps that's why it survived.

There a 'No Cycling' sign on the Roman Road, and you'll fall off if you try. Goodness knows what the chariots made of it. However, you might want to pose for a picture on it: after all, this may be one of only three original Roman road surfaces you can put a bicycle on.

Find your way back to the circular

> *Goodness knows what the chariots made of it*

trail and dawdle your way through the forest to the bike centre for a cup of tea, and cycle back to Lydney in due course.

■ Also in the area

The Forest of Dean area is lovely to cycle around. It's cool and shady when the weather is hot, crisp and tranquil when it's misty-cold and atmospheric when it's rainy. The B roads here can be busy and unpleasant (and hilly), and the narrow minor roads a delight, threading through hills, woods and trim villages with excellent refreshment opportunities. Most people will be quite happy to stick to the car-free trails though. Wild boar are said to be thriving in the Forest of Dean

Symond's Yat is only a few kilometres north-west of the bike centre. This stretch of the Wye Valley, between the Danube-like panorama off the rock promontory at Symond's Yat and down to Chepstow, offers some of the most spectacular river-valley scenery in the UK. There are also some interesting little ferry crossings for cyclists *(see page 78)*. It's not easy or flat cycling to get there, though, and the only route along most of the Wye is a fast main road.

A few kilometres' train ride down from Lydney is Chepstow. From here, a branch of Sustrans' Lôn Las Cymru (Welsh National Cycle Route, also National Cycle Route 42) runs

up through Hay-on-Wye and then through Wales to Holyhead. A family-friendly cycle route from Chepstow to Tintern Abbey is said to be in preparation. National Cycle Route 4, from London to west Wales, passes over the old Severn Bridge *(cyclable, of course: see page 161)* and through Chepstow.

■ Other places like this

Wade's Causeway (OS 94, grid ref SE809983) is in fabulous cycling country near Goathland, in the North York Moors *(see also Chimney Bank on page 150, and the North York Moors Railway on page 162)*. South of the village are many signposts to the 'Roman Road (footpath)'. Cycling is prohibited and anyway would be extremely unpleasant. An information board informs you that experts believe the road to be (a) post-Roman, (b) pre-Roman, or else (c) Roman.

Blackstone Edge (OS 109, grid ref SD980174) is cyclable (by MTBs), and scenically impressive *(pictured on page 120)*. But it's very inconvenient to get to, not part of any obvious ride. It's just south of the A58 west from Halifax, east of Blackstone Edge Reservoir. A bridleway branches south-west off the main road, onto Rishworth Moor, and right onto the old Roman Road surface: a rocky, cobbled, astonishingly well-preserved track (though some dispute its age). The long, deep-worn central groove was for pole brakes.

There is a surviving 3rd-century Roman arch which you can cycle underneath in Lincoln. Newport Arch is on the north side of Lincoln, on the way out of town on the old Ermine St. To get there, follow Steep Hill due north from the centre; it continues as Bailgate and Newport taking you to the arch, although some parts are one-way in the wrong direction. The low headroom is deceptive: the actual road surface was a metre or two lower in those days.

Snackstop

Picnic. *There's a succession of picnic sites off the B road around over a kilometre north/west of Blackpool Bridge.*

Bevvy break

Miners Arms, Whitecroft. *Not far from Parkend is this excellent source of real ale, particularly CAMRA-award-winning cider and perry. Skittle alley, boules court and outdoor tables.*

Quirkshop

Clearwell Caves, south of Coleford and about 8km due west of Blackpool Bridge, is an ancient natural cave system that you can visit (£5 adults).

Tourer's tick list

✓ Dean Forest Railway
✓ Cycle forest trails

OS 162, grid ref SO 652088
INFO Dean Heritage Centre, Camp Mill, Soudley GL14 2UB,
tel: 01594 822170,
www.deanheritagemuseum.com

Historic Harlech Castle
(conveniently near Pen Llech)

FFORD PEN LLECH

WHERE *Gwynedd, Wales: Harlech to Porthmadog (12km)*

WHAT *Road riding by thrilling coast scenery*

WHY *Tackle Britain's steepest road, a strange bridge, and Portmeirion*

HOW *Train to Harlech, train back from Porthmadog*

This short trip between train stations along main roads in the far north-west of Wales gives you some amazing experiences en route; if you want to extend the riding, you can add some flat kilometres to go further north. As well as the strangely dreamlike village of Portmeirion, you also tackle Britain's steepest road.

Britain's steepest road: a 40% plunge by the castle

From Harlech train station, head the short distance towards Harlech Castle, spectacularly situated on a high outcrop overlooking the waters. Turn at the second left up Twtil, a impossibly steep hill up round the castle that takes you to Harlech's High St. Now turn immediately left back down the hill: this is Fford Pen Llech, the nearest you'll get on a British road to downhill skiing on a bike. The narrow strip of tarmac careers down between cottages as if in a panic. According to the Guinness Book of Records, as it was called in the days when it listed such things, this is Britain's steepest road. The sign at the top starkly describes its gradient as 40%, or 1 in 2.5. Guinness maintained it is only 34%, or 1 in 2.91. Such figures are only a rough guide, because the angle of the surface varies so much during its pinball-like progress. At any rate, for most of its descent it's too steep for comfort. The most extreme point - the inside crook of the last hairpin - may be as much as 50%, to judge by the pictures taken

on our special expedition.

Ffordd Pen Llech means something like 'Bluff Head Road'; in English it is referred to as 'Llech Hill'. It is marked *Anaddas i fodur – Unsuitable for motors*. This doesn't seem to deter local car drivers from slaloming their way down. It's also marked as a one-way street the downwards way, but you will see the odd vehicle struggling upwards.

You do see local cyclists taking on this tarmac flume. On our investigation we encountered two but could apprehend neither for an interview before they warp-factored off down into the distance. Locals tell you the road's one-eighty turns regularly propel Merioneth's over-ambitious cycling youth over the low walls into nettled thickets.

According to the tourist information office, Ffordd Pen Llech used to be the main route through the town. Mums from the village nonchalantly walk their baby buggies up and down it. Harlech's celebrated castle - an awesome sight, especially from down below - is worth visiting, as

armies have done through history. It's seen geological battles too: the sea came up to the bottom of the cliff when it was built, but now the shoreline has receded half a mile. Had you hurtled down Ffordd Pen Llech on a bicycle in the 13th century , you'd have ended up in the sea.

You do see local cyclists taking on this tarmac flume

Of Harlech's 1200-odd inhabitants, around two-thirds speak Welsh. Hang around when some of the kids fall off their bikes going down the hill and you'll learn some useful colloquial phrases.

Follow the A496 north-east, a fast and unpleasant road that takes you across a small bridge and past the puffing steam trains of Ffestiniog Railway. On the left you see the entrance to Portmeirion. The film-set-like Italianate village was the setting for the 1960s TV series The Prisoner, and bikes are the ideal way to enjoy it. For an unforgettable experience you can stay here in Portmeirion's hotel, especially if your accountant has advised you to devise a large and urgent tax loss.

Continue to Porthmadog across a remarkable little causeway, The Cob, which the heritage railway's locos also chug across. Mainline trains run from Porthmadog (and back to Harlech in 20 minutes).

The extraordinary Barmouth Bridge *(see page 134)* is 16km to the south. One branch of the long-distance Lôn Las Cymru, the fantastic Sustrans Welsh National Cycle Route running from Cardiff to Holyhead *(aka National Cycle Route 8; see pages 128 & 136)*, links the bridge with Harlech.

From Porthmadog you might like to cycle on north on NCR 8, to Caernarfon (45km from Porthmadog) over the historic Menai Suspension Bridge (12km from Caernarfon) to Anglesey. Around 30km of this stretch is nice flat rail trail. Immediately past the Menai Bridge is a photo-opportunity for cyclists with wide angle lenses, by posing in front of one of the many signboards in the village of Llanfairpwllgwyngyllgogerychwyrndrobwllllantysiliogogogoch. The name is easy to pronounce, because like all Welsh, it is pronounced as it is spelt. Ferries run from Holyhead to Dublin.

A 20-minute train ride from Bangor (by the Menai Bridge) takes you to Conwy on the north coast, home of the smallest house in Britain and a castle; the cycle ride round the head at Llandudno, on to Colwyn Bay, and then a joyous 25km all along the promenade to Prestatyn, is something really special. Combine that with the Harlech bit described above, perhaps staying overnight in Caernarfon, for a weekend trip.

■ Also in the area

This is Snowdonia, so it's tough but very rewarding cycling country for the adventurous sort with maps.

■ Other places like this

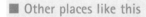

In Ramsbottom, Lancashire, the kilometre-long Rawson's Rake averages 'only' 1 in 5, but is the course for the national cycle hill climbing championships. In Swansea, the mile-long ascent of Constitution Hill - with its stretches of 1 in 3 - is said to be 'Britain's steepest cobbled urban road-traffic street'.

Bristol's tumbledown district of Totterdown has a steeper (albeit uncobbled) street. The bottom few metres of Vale St *(pictured, right)*, near Bristol Temple Meads station, are somewhere around 43%-45%, though strangely there are no 'steep hill' signs. It resembles a vertical drawbridge, or tarmac launching-pad for STOL aircraft, sandwiched by steps. From the bottom it fills the horizon. The street is about 100m long, with houses raked up both sides, and cars parked almost perpendicular to jam them against the kerb in case they slide down in the middle of the night. Photographic evidence suggests that its gradient here supports the otherwise scarcely credible claim of 1 in 2.4.

In north-east Bath, not far from Bristol, there are several extremely steep streets just off London Road; try the near-vertical Bennett's Lane or Frankley Buildings, but not on an icy day. These, apparently, are the routine first assignments for rookie postal workers.

The 'official' world record holder for the world's steepest street is Baldwin St, Dunedin's asphalt ski slope in New Zealand. Its maximum of only 1 in 2.91, or 38%, is not as big as Vale St's extreme, and is considerably less than Fford Pen Llech's. It's longer and steeper than either overall, however.

Snackstop

Cemlyn Restaurant, High St, Harlech. *Big range of proper teas and coffee, and views of castle and mountains.*

Bevvy break

Lion Hotel, Harlech. *Traditional olde inne in the old town.*

Quirkshop

This is a good place to hear glorious gutturals and sparkling sibilants of ancient, poetic Welsh. Try dau beint o gwrw plîs (dye baeent o guru pleece) - 'two pints of beer please'. Or yr wyf yn mwynhau beicio fel hamdden, pleser ac ymarfer corff (ur wiv un mooinhigh bikey-o vel ham then, plezer ac umarver corf) - 'I enjoy biking for leisure, enjoyment and exercise'. Or beth os syrthia i? (beth oss seertheea ee) - 'what if I fall off?'

Tourer's tick list

✓ Harlech Castle
✓ Coast/hill views from town, espesially at sunset
✓ Ffestiniog railway
✓ Portmeirion
✓ Forest trails in Coed-y-Brenin
✓ Lôn Las Cymru

OS 124, grid ref SH5831
INFO Harlech Tourist Information, 46 High St, Harlech Ll46 2YE, tel. 01766 780658

TRANSPORTER BRIDGES

WHERE   *Gwent, Wales: Newport to Blaenavon (24km one way)*

WHAT   *Traffic-free trail along old canal*

WHY   *Go by Transporter Bridge, one of only six in the world*

HOW   *Train to Newport*

This beautiful, well-surfaced, reasonably easy traffic-free path - Route 46 on the National Cycle Network - takes you from Newport Castle, mostly on canal towpaths, almost imperceptibly up the valleys to Blaenavon. And a 3km detour south at the start gives you the chance to enjoy an experience you can do at only six places in the world: take your bike on a transporter bridge, a kind of flying fox for vehicles.

A bridge? A ferry? A lift? and one of only six in the world

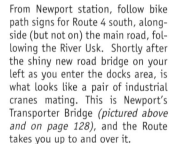

From Newport station, follow bike path signs for Route 4 south, alongside (but not on) the main road, following the River Usk. Shortly after the shiny new road bridge on your left as you enter the docks area, is what looks like a pair of industrial cranes mating. This is Newport's Transporter Bridge *(pictured above and on page 128)*, and the Route takes you up to and over it.

Apparently made from leftovers of the Eiffel Tower flatpack, it has no road deck - only a platform the size of a tennis court suspended from its towers. It shuttles 174m across from one bank to the other like an Edwardian fairground ride or scrap-metal magic carpet. The TB runs from 8am-5.50pm Mon-Sat, and 1pm- 4.50pm Sun; cars are 50p, bikes free. It's an odd feeling, as the platform, with its handful of cars, passengers and the odd cyclist, glides gently across over water. There you are on a turquoise end-of-the-pier, suddenly detached from its moorings and heading off across the water like something from a Raymond Briggs cartoon. You hover in mundane splendour over finest Welsh silt in a panorama of dockland tundra. Then you're at the other side, the barriers lift, and off you cycle. There isn't much to do on the other side except buy a bag of crisps and wait to cross back.

TBs enjoyed a brief vogue a century ago, the first example being in Portugalete, Spain, in 1893. They were thought a useful solution for the handful of places which were impractical for ferries (due to shifting sands, treacherous tides and currents) conventional bridges (high clearance needed, but perhaps no space for long approach roads in the built-up areas either side) and tunnels (expense). By 1916, 16 of them had been built in places of cutting-edge fashion such as Marseille, Buenos Aires, Rio de Janeiro, Widnes and Warrington. But they proved uneconomic for growing traffic volumes, and most of them closed.

Only half a dozen remain in use: in Rochefort, France; Rendsburg and Osten, Germany; Portugalete; and - cheeringly - our very own Newport and Middlesborough. (Warrington's is disused; Widnes's was scrapped in

railway line, and go across a spectacular viaduct outside Blaenavon. If you don't want to cycle all 24km back to Newport station, you can get a train there from Pontypool, halfway back.

■ Also in the area

There are two other neat bridges with cycle provision over the Usk in Newport town centre. Fans of those nails-and-string sculptures will be enjoy cycling across George St bridge, a road bridge with separate pedestrian and cycle lanes, which was Britain's first cable-stayed bridge in 1964. Right in the centre is the impressive new pedestrian/cycle-only crossing, Newport City Footbridge, which looks as though it's held in place by a crane. It opened for business on the day of the TB's centenary, 12 Sep 2006.

1961.) Newport's was opened in 1906 as a showpiece TB - or trasbordeur, as the French designer Ferdinand Arnodin called it, trying to inject a little romantic interest into his 73m-high fusewire washing-line. It never made money, and was closed in 1985 as unsafe, but reopened in 1995.

Retrace your steps back to Newport centre, but keep on north following Route 46 for 24km. You go past the castle along the banks of the Usk, and are guided over to join a canal. From here you're on towpaths of the Monmouthshire Canal, and the lovely Monmouthshire & Brecon Canal, almost all the way to the end. Some parts are derelict, some being restored, and others lively with narrowboaters, and there's a lot of superb scenery en route. From near Pontypool you're mostly on an old

like an Edwardian fairground ride or scrap-metal magic carpet

Just a short hop on a train away, starting from Cardiff, is the fabulous Lôn Las Cymru - Sustrans' Wales End-to-End. It makes a splendid week or so's tour. The Taff Trail, National Cycle Route 8, goes from Cardiff to Brecon and Hay-on-Wye.

A train also takes you to Chepstow, an alternative starting point for the LLC, or a hopping-off point for the Severn Bridge crossing *(see page 161)*. You might also take a train to Lydney to ride the Forest of Dean and see the unique original Roman road at Blackpool

Bridge *(see page 118)*.

National Cycle Route 4, on the Welsh coast from London to St David's, goes by the Transporter Bridge. National Cycle Routes 46 and 47 run from Newport to Neath and Fishguard respectively.

■ Other places like this

Middlesbrough's TB *(page 126, main picture)*, built in 1911, is a bit longer (177m) than Newport's, and just as enjoyable (though it charges bikes 50p per crossing). It's also much bluer, and certainly easier to find: from the railway station simply head north 400m to the big Transporter Bridge Shaped Thing. Middlesbrough is at the end of Sustrans White Rose route, which starts 200km away in Hull. It's much nicer than it sounds, and you go through the solar system en-route *(see page 166)*. The last few kilometres of the route, as you head through the downtrodden urban parkland, towards Middlesbrough, are ruined by endless swathes of broken glass. The photogenic end point of the White Rose route is in the centre of Middlesborough, by a sculpture of a giant bottle, which may be an ironic comment.

Warrington's rather stumpy transporter, which formerly shuttled 57m across the Mersey, has been dormant since 1964; it's still there and Grade II listed, but is in poor condition.

London has a potential transporter bridge: the 127m metal framework bridge over Victoria Dock, just east of Docklands. It's next to ExCeL, the exhibition hall, and links the north side of the docks with the residential area on the south. It was conceived as a Transporter Bridge, with a small glass passenger kiosk sliding across a parabolic curved rail fixed on the underside of the deck. As things stand, it's foot passengers only, who go up in a lift and walk across the top.

Snackstop
Hunky Dorys, Charles St, Newport. *There's nothing around the Transporter Bridge so you'll have to picnic, or go into the town centre. We hear good things about this place.*

Bevvy break
Open Hearth, Sebastopol, Pontypool. *Little country pub right on the towpath just a couple of kilometres south of Pontypool rail station with decent cask beer*

Quirkshop
The Ryder Cup - the two-yearly golf challenge between Europe and the US which Europe always seems to win nowadays - comes to Newport in 2010, at the upmarket Celtic Manor Resort.

Tourer's tick list
✓ Cycle George St bridge, City Footbridge
✓ Viaduct at Blaenavon
✓ Scenery on Monmouthshire & Brecon Canal
✓ Big Pit Mining Museum

OS 171, grid ref ST317863/ 93, grid ref NZ500214

INFO Newport Tourist Information Centre, John Frost Sq, Newport NP20 1PA, tel. 01633 842962, newport.tic@newport.gov.uk; Bridge Visitor Centre 01633 250322, open Sat/Sun

Pontcysyllte

PONTCYSYLLTE

WHERE   *Chirk, Clwyd, Wales: Circular ride through Llangollen (30km)*

WHAT   *Canal towpaths and a few steep lanes*

WHY   *Great panorama, and Pontcysyllte's astounding flying canal*

HOW   *Train to Chirk*

his circular ride, on flat towpaths and a few steep lanes, gives you one of Britain's most remarkable engineering feats - the flying horse-trough of Pontcysyllte aqueduct that leaps across the River Dee outside Llangollen - as well as a stunning panorama and characterful towns.

Britain's most aerial walkway.
Historic and unfenced

From Chirk, head north from the station through the town. Join the canal towpath when you can, at Pentre. At Pontcysyllte car park, peek at the aqueduct if you like, but come off down on the road (signposted Trevor) that crosses the River Dee directly under the aqueduct. It's impressive enough to look up at - just wait till you're on top of it.

Carry on to Pontcysyllte, past the Telford Inn. A left and right take you to Garth, from where you follow the sign for the panorama, a place true to its word: the views of the Dee valley and surrounding hills is stunning. Past Castell Dinas Bran turn left and go down over the canal into the busy town of Llangollen. In July, when the musical eisteddfod is on, it'll be even busier. From Llangollen return to the canal and join the towpath, heading back towards the aqueduct. At the basin you turn right, and now the fun really begins.

Crossing the aqueduct is more like a tightrope walk than a canalside stroll. In 2005, Thomas Telford's remarkable structure celebrated 200 years of scaring the crap out of people. The exquisite sense of mid-air vertigo comes from being on something so thin (under 3m wide), so long (over 300m, Britain's longest canal aqueduct) and so high above the valley floor (38m), with a guardrail on one side only (the towpath side, fortunately). It looks so damn house-of-cards precarious, with a towpath barely wide enough for a full set of toes.

Pontcysyllte is a celebrated item in any repertoire of travel stories. Talk to any narrowboaters and they'll have a story about crossing it, and another story they heard about someone else who crossed it. It is perfectly safe, of course, so long as you follow the rules. Cycling the towpath on either side of the aqueduct is perfectly OK, but a bilingual notice at both ends clearly informs you that cycling, horses and abseiling are all prohibited on the stretch of the aqueduct itself. So don't let your horse abseil down on a bicycle. And, obviously, don't copy the locals who cycle across nonchalantly with one hand, texting their friends with the other and weaving through the walking sightseeers.

Spend some time in the middle. Savour the views and the to-ing and

on the BBC website somewhere, but viewing is not recommended for those with a weak bladder.

Carry on along the towpath to return to the road that brought you in from Chirk.

■ Also in the area

If you arrive by taking the train to Chirk, it's worth nosing around the canal just south of the station. There's a narrow towpath (no cycling, so push instead) through the 459m Chirk Tunnel (lights are very useful here). On the other side, you're straight onto the Chirk Aqueduct, which is smaller, but nearly as spectacular.

There's an impressive castle a couple of kilometres west of Chirk from where you get fine views of the surrounding countryside and

fro-ing of people and water traffic. Boats somehow don't belong that far up in the air, and a narrowboat, squeezing across (there's only a few centimetres of clearance either side) is an exciting sight. Not as exciting as it must be to sit on your boat and peer over the lip of the trough only a couple of centimetres above water level, vertiginously down to the fields and the river, a long way below. Boats are fairly frequent as this may be the most scenic stretch of canal in the country, and is

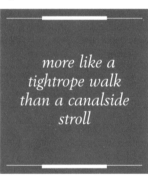

more like a tightrope walk than a canalside stroll

the Ceiriog valley - in other words it's uphill. In general, the countryside round here is very scenic, and crossed by lots of steep country lanes, making for attractive but strenuous cycling.

In Llangollen, the beautiful heritage railway (www.llangollen-railway.co.uk)

very popular with cruisers. To enhance the feeling of the aqueduct being the world's widest lavatory cistern, there is a plug at the bottom, about halfway across. In 2002 it was pulled so as to drain the trough for maintenance, resulting in a half-hour flush of its contents down to the River Dee beneath. There are vivid pictures of the event

runs steam trains all summer, and most weekends the rest of the year, up the Dee valley to Carrog, half an hour away. They have nice big guards vans and for an extra £1 they will take bicycles. You might want to cycle along the riverside lane that follows the north side to Carrog and take the train back.

National Cycle Route 5 (Reading to Holyhead via the north Wales coast) runs through Chester, which is a short distance up the rail line from Chirk.

■ Other places like this

As is mentioned above, Chirk Aqueduct is on the same canal, just a few kilometres to the south of Pontcysyllte.

The two most beautiful canal aqueducts on the waterways are between Bath and Bradford *(see page 18)* while one of the most surprising is found in London *(see page 66)*.

Pontcysyllte is one of the 'Seven Wonders of the Waterways' as listed in an important 1946 book on canals, written by Robert Aickman. Two of the others, Caen Hill Locks just outside Devizes *(see page 30)* and Five Rise Locks outside Bingley *(see page 33)*, are fine cycling experiences, either as neat little day trips on their own, or as parts of longer canalside tours. Burnley Embankment is a 1.5km-long, straight, high embankment over Burnley town centre. Although it's not quite as visually impressive as Pontcysyllte from the towpath, it can be cycled as part of a Leeds-Liverpool Canal ride, and it does also have an aqueduct. The other three Wonders of the Waterways - Anderton Boat Lift, Standedge Tunnel, and Barton Swing Aqueduct - aren't practical cycling experiences, unless you can cadge a lift from someone.

The aqueduct over the River Lune up in Lancaster is pretty impressive - a big stone bridge by John Rennie - but there aren't many stretches of this particular canal towpath you're allowed to cycle.

Snackstop
Llangollen railway station. *The main station - in fact, the only station - on this eight-mile restored heritage railway has a cafe and a picnic area by the river. It's in the town centre just down from the canal.*

Bevvy break
Telford Inn, north side of aqueduct. *Average sort of pub with usual range of keg beers and grub, but well situated overlooking canal basin and with lots of outside tables.*

Quirkshop
According to the British Waterways website, "on moonlit nights an eerie figure can be seen gliding along the towpath" across the aqueduct.

Tourer's tick list
✓ Llangollen
✓ Steam railway
✓ Chirk Tunnel
✓ Panorama
✓ Two castles

OS 117, grid ref SJ270421
INFO Llangollen Tourist Information, Centre Y Chapel, Castle St, Llangollen LL20 8NU,
tel. 01978 860828, llangollen@nwtic.com

BARMOUTH BRIDGE

WHERE *Gwynedd, Wales: Barmouth to Dolgellau (15km one way)*

WHAT *Canal towpaths and a few steep lanes*

WHY *Great panorama, and Pontcysyllte's astounding flying canal*

HOW *Train to Barmouth*

This is the Llwybr Mawddach (Mawddach Trail): a flat, family-friendly, car-free day ride alongside a beautiful estuary under Cader Idris, taking you 15km from the seaside resort of Barmouth to the characterful town of Dolgellau. It also includes a unique experience: the ride across an amazing 800m wooden bridge.

Bracing, wooden, car-free traverse of a big estuary

From Barmouth (Welsh, *Abermaw*) station, head south a hundred metres or so to the mouth of the Mawddach estuary. Before you is the sight of Barmouth Bridge, reassuringly clanky and wooden, more like an ancient pleasure pier than a river crossing, the sort that should have a What the Butler Saw machine at the end. From the main road a smooth tarmac access path runs sharply downhill. Whizz down here to the tollbooth, where you pay your 70p toll (60p for you, 10p for the bike; the return is free).

For the cyclist it's a delight. You share its 820m length only with pedestrians and the occasional mainline train – cars have a 20km round trip up the estuary and back. Second, as you rumble across this giant matchstick model, you have the bracing feeling of being out at sea. You're in the middle of quite an imposing landscape – Cader Idris, which is about as high as the bridge is long, is one of the mountain tops that faces Barmouth town across the water. It can get pretty windy out in the middle, so hold on to anything potentially airworthy, unless you're an oceanologist wanting to know where your hat will wash ashore in Newfoundland. Third, because bike pace is just right for appreciating this remarkable piece of tree-based engineering.

For the first few dozen metres on the bridge you go alongside its two coathanger steel spans. You then dip down a step onto the long main section, made up of sleeper-sized

chunks of wood laid crossways, supported by a forest of wooden piles. The planks, warped by generations of briny spray, don't quite fit, and clank as you cycle over them – making Barmouth Bridge also the world's biggest xylophone.

The structure was opened in 1867, with a wooden drawbridge section that opened to let tall ships pass. That was replaced in 1901 by the two steel spans. These can still swing to let vessels through, but they're rarely called on to do so nowadays. A bridge made of logs

can face peculiar problems: this one was closed for repairs in the 1980s when they found that it was being eaten by worms.

Head off left immediately after the bridge to follow the old railway line alongside the estuary. At Penmaenpool, an old signal box has been converted into a birdwatching hut. There's another charming, but much shorter, restored wooden toll bridge across the estuary here (which cars can use). Carry on for a couple more kilometres to Dolgellau, and return at leisure to Barmouth back the way you came.

Barmouth is a traditional British beach resort, although with a touch of something special about it thanks to the bridge, the estuary, the scenery and the sunsets. Here you can stock up on vital supplies of fish and chips,  *the world's biggest xylophone* swimming costumes, snowstorm paperweights, and a bucket and spade. There are several pubs, cafes and places to stay too. Sad to say, Barmouth biscuits – delicious thin round cookies resembling French langues de chat that were a favourite of our grandmothers – mysteriously vanished at the same time as Betamax video.

■ Also in the area

A steady climb from Dolgellau offers some views as a reward. Head west-south-west from Dolgellau following signs for Cader Idris / National Cycle Network Route 8. The 10km uphill (200m, so it's not too bad) has increasingly impressive views of the estuary. Turn right at the sign for Llynnau Cregennon lakes down a steep lane. Turn left onto the main road, and after 400m go right down the track; this rejoins the Mawddach trail – turn left back to Barmouth and the bridge.

John Ruskin, who clearly should have run guided cycle tours, said that only one journey in the world has views to compare with those of Dolgellau to Barmouth: that of Barmouth to Dolgellau. A summer ferry takes foot passengers from Barmouth to Fairbourne, from where a miniature railway runs parallel to the big bridge, but neither ferry nor train takes bikes. However, you can make the round trip to Fairbourne by coming over the bridge and turning right.

From Barmouth you can follow the Lôn Las Cymru (Welsh National Cycle Route) north about 18k to Harlech *(see page 122)*. Depending on the tide, half of it can be ridden along the beach, avoiding a main road. Be warned that Welsh sand is as effective as any for infiltrating socks, sandwiches, and the hitherto oily bits of bicycles. The LLC also has a branch from Dolgellau north up to Porthmadog, missing out Harlech. That way goes through Coed-y-Brenin forest, a mountain biker's favourite with dozens of routes.

■ Other places like this

The Cob, at Porthmadog 30km or so north up the LLC from Barmouth *(see page 134)* is scenically similar, though the trail is shared with a main road as well as a railway.

The closest you'll get to replicating Barmouth Bridge's timber-framed traverse is probably on an old-style pleasure pier rather than a bridge. Most of the UK's bigger piers – such as the world's longest at Southend – tend to catch fire, collapse in storms, and worst of all, prohibit bicycles. But in Ryde, on the Isle of Wight, you can enjoy the clanky-plank experience. Take your bike on the hovercraft to the Isle from Portsmouth (£16.40 return, bikes free), arrive at the head of Ryde Pier and get to dry land by biking along the 703m long wooden surface *(pictured right)*. We believe Ryde's is the longest pier in the UK to allow cycling; those at Southend (2158m) Southport (1107m) and Walton-on-the-Naze (792m) don't.

Other well-known wooden bridges in England include the old toll bridge in Selby, except it's not wooden any more, and the footbridge to Queens College, Cambridge; still wooden, but not cyclable except as an ill-advised student stunt. The ancient wooden toll bridge over the River Adur in Shoreham, Sussex, is cyclable, and well used, just south of the A27, by the Red Lion pub. Various bits now are made of iron, and the surface is tarmac, but at heart it remains a horizontal tree.

Snackstop
Mermaid Fish Bar, Jubilee Rd, Barmouth. *Well-regarded traditional chippy – even does deep-fried Mars Bars.*

Bevvy break
The Last Inn, near the harbour, Barmouth. *Atmospheric 15th-century pub. The mountainside forms one of the walls with a mountain spring running down and a pond with fish. Views out over the water. Real ale, generous food.*

Quirkshop
Take a photo of yourself in front of the Carousel Cafe in Barmouth. The initial letter C on the signboard has been stolen so many times that the owner has given up replacing it. It is therefore now the AROUSAL CAFE.

Tourer's tick list
✓ Panorama point 1km north-west of bridge
✓ Birdwatching
✓ Barmouth beach, swim, ice-cream
✓ Cycle promenade, then north along beach

OS 124, grid ref SH619155
INFO Tourist Info, Old Library, Station Road, Barmouth LL42 1LU, tel. 01341 280787, barmouth.tic@gwynedd.gov.uk (summer only)

ASHBOURNE TUNNEL

WHERE   *Derbyshire: Cromford to Parsley Hay to Ashbourne (40km one way)*

WHAT   *Flat, scenic, car-free rail trail gem*

WHY   *Ends in unique ghost-train tunnel experience*

HOW   *Train to Cromford*

This takes you along two excellent traffic-free, mostly flat, easy-going rail trails through pleasant Peaks scenery: the High Peak Trail and the Tissington Trail, which join at Parsley Hay. And in the tunnel at the end, the route offers a curious sound experience, unique in Britain.

A spooky experience to round off the lovely Tissington Trail

Start from Cromford station, just south of Matlock. Head over the river and go a couple of kilometres up the steepish busy road through the town of Cromford. (The only road component of the trip.) Just after the road forks left, take the left into the car park and picnic area. This is your access to the High Peak trail. Once you've made the initial ascent of a series of large shallow steps, the trail runs pretty flat across the top of the peaks along an old railway to Parsley Hay. Scenery here is unspectacular but there is some quite interesting old rail engineering.

Parsley Hay is about 20km from Cromford, so you're about halfway. It feels quite remote up here, although it isn't really – and there is a cafe. Here is where the two rail trails meet. You want to turn sharp left, down the Tissington Trail. This is another fabulous Sustrans delight, part of the mammoth National Cycle Route 68 which runs up the spine of England (see below). It's deservedly popular, and on a school holiday will be well-plied with families out on a day's cycle. From here the scenery gets better with some impressive cuttings and embankments, and views of Dovedale. There are also regular but discreet cafes and snack opportunities (and toilets) at the old stations between here and Ashbourne, belying the away-from-it-all feeling. It runs slightly downhill to Ashbourne but not so much that you'd notice.

You know you've arrived at Ashbourne when the tunnel appears: 350m of nicely-restored, well-lit, old rail tunnel. It isn't the longest railtrail tunnel – Staple Hill's is over 470m – but it's possibly the quirkiest, for reasons connected with soundscapes. Bathrooms turn most of us into a would-be Luciano Pavarotti; railtrail tunnels make us into Thomas the Tank Engine. Few cyclists, on entering the reverberant pipeline soundscape, can resist making the whistle of a steam loco, the sound of wheels

clattering over a points spaghetti, or the howl of a passenger who leaned just a bit too far out the window. But here, someone else got there first. Because this is one of Sustrans' many imaginative and original art installations. As you cycle through the tunnel, recordings of ghostly trains, slamming doors and chattering passengers echo around in a deliciously unsettling way.

Even though you know there can

■ Also in the area...

Ashbourne is on the Sustrans Pennine Cycleway (National Cycle Route 68) which goes 570km from Derby to Berwick-on-Tweed, so, if you want to head south, NCN68 will lead you on quiet roads the 20km or so to Derby, from where you can catch the train.

From Parsley Hay, the High Peak Trail runs on north-west towards Buxton, 20km or so away. It doesn't make it all the way, so you have to ride the last few kilometres on road. Buxton is well worth a visit in its own right, and it has a mainline rail station (though on a completely different line to Cromford: cumbersome changes mean it's three hours by train from Buxton to Cromford, so it's actually quicker to cycle back).

be no trains – there are no rails for one thing, and there's probably a Ford Fiesta parked across one of the tunnel entrances – you still find yourself glancing nervously behind you. Those with Ivor the Engine-related paranoid delusions are advised to steer clear.

Just out the other side is a convenient pub to refresh yourself. Ashbourne town centre is up to your left. The most convenient way back to Cromford is back the way you came; there isn't another railway station any nearer to Ashbourne, and it's too much to do the return trip in one day, so your best bet is to stay overnight in Ashbourne and return to Cromford the next day. Or you can continue south from Ashbourne, on road, to Derby – see below.

railtrail tunnels make us into Thomas the Tank Engine

There are plenty of cycle hire facilities on these trails, at Ashbourne, Parsley Hay and Middleton Top (for details, see www.derbyshire-peakdistrict.co.uk /cycling.htm), making this area ideal if you can't or don't want to take your own bikes – or if want to try a tandem.

The shorter Manifold Trail and Monsal trail nearby are scenic too.

From Cromford, scenic Matlock is only a few kilometres north, but it's either along a busy and fast main road by the river, or the hilltop back road. There's a pleasant, picnicky canal in Cromford Wharf, but the towpath is not for cyclists.

Mam Tor's 'earthquake road' is not far away, and there's an enjoyably deep ford to splash through on a summer's day *(see page 142)*.

■ Other places like this

For more on cyclable tunnels, see the entry on Staple Hill on page 22, and also the one on the Tyne Tunnel on page 174.

Sustrans' website is the place to go (www.sustrans. org) to find rail trails similar to the Tissington or High Peak. There are many dozens of similar routes round the country, and almost certainly a few near where you live. Many of their routes specialise in trailside installations, ranging from the stunning to the quirky, and there are countless examples around the UK. Virtually any Sustrans route near you will have some interesting things installed along the way. Most of them are sculptures; but Ashbourne Tunnel's sonic drama is, as far as we know, unique as a per-

manent feature. Sustrans' website has a page on their recent installation projects. We particularly like their cyclable maze at Consett *(see page 178)*.

Of course, for real sonic tunnel drama, simply go into a tunnel that's either full of actual traffic trying to run you over (such as Queensway Tunnel under the Mersey, or Rotherhithe Tunnel under the Thames) or full of ghosts in your head *(see page 114)*. But we suspect that you'll find the Ashbourne experience much more pleasant.

Snackstop
Old Coach House Tearoom, Tissington Hall. *In the village of Tissington, a few metres west of the trail; everyone we know who's been has recommended it.*

Bevvy break
Coach & Horses, Fenny Bentley. *Charming 16th-century coaching house in a village with outside tables for summer, fire inside for winter, and decent meals. It's about 3km north of Ashbourne, about 1km east of the trail.*

Quirkshop
Each year on Shrove Tuesday and Ash Wednesday, Ashbourne is the site of what is claimed to be the world's oldest football match. Half of the town plays the other half in a day-long mad scramble, using the whole town as a pitch.

Tourer's tick list
✓ Buxton
✓ Matlock
✓ Cromford Canal

OS 119, grid ref SK176469
INFO Ashbourne Tourist Informtion, 13 Market Place Ashbourne DE6 1EU, tel. 01335 343666, ashbourneinfo@derbyshiredales.gov.uk; http://vs2.i-dat.org/unstructured02 /sound.html

The gentle slope
of sunny
Mam Tor

MAM TOR

WHERE   *Derbyshire: Hope to Mam Tor (10km round trip)*

WHAT   *Roads and disused roads in Peaks scenery*

WHY   *Bizarre surface warped into roller-coaster by landslips*

HOW   *Train to Hope station*

his short, rugged road ride in the Peaks takes you onto something that looks more like an earthquake zone: 2km of extraordinary shattered tarmac on Mam Tor. You can easily add on a 30km largely traffic-free ride that takes in Britain's best reservoir cycle circuit to make a fabulous full day trip.

The shivering mountain that beat the road-builders

From Hope station head west along the main road through Castleton, past the shops and pubs. Instead of branching left up the 'main' road over Winnats Pass, which machetes its way through the hills to your left, stay straight on. This is a cul-de-sac, used as a car park by those walking on Mam Tor, the hill to your right. The road soon bends right, starts to rise, and (at an intriguing sign saying 'beware of live traffic') a gate bars motorised traffic from going further.

You soon see why. Until 1977, this was the A625, the main road across the Peaks from Sheffield. It made its way confidently out the town, turning right, up, and then sharp left, to hairpin its way calmly over the flank of Mam Tor. But the restless hillside is composed of horizontal layers of shale, and when they get wet, they slide across each other like a pile of trays spilt by an overambitious waiter. That year, storms – brutally contradicting the previous parched summer – saturated the mountain; the fragile surface broke up, and the road was pulled apart like a landslipped Andean pass in highest Bolivia. Repair proved impossible; the authorities gave up, closed it, and let the road crumble gradually down the hillside. It's now tarmac blancmange, and we cyclists have it all to ourselves.

In a couple of places the road surface breaks up and drops away, evidence of why it would now cost an estimated £100,000 a year to maintain. Past the hairpin, the plasticine

peak does its most dramatic stuff. For a hundred metres or more the road is squashed, torn apart and ripped up, its entrails gruesomely displayed. At some points, fault-line shears expose a cross-section of the road's lavishly-layered structure. It still wasn't enough to resist the 'shivering mountain'.

At the greatest drop-off, a sheer wall the height of an ambulance shows why this stretch of abandoned road is best cycled uphill. Coming down, you could easily fail to see it. The scenery's pretty good, too. On the right, climbing up, there is a ridge flecked with walkers; Edale is on the other side.

Soon you arrive at another gate, and back to the spur of stable, motorable surface that returns you to the main road. From here, make sure that your brake blocks are healthy and go left and left. This is Winnats Pass, plunging over 200m in around 2km, with stretches of 1 in 5. This is the old road that the

to sit out the downpour in a coffee shop or a tavern, in company with perhaps some of the dissolving walkers who themselves were huddled in tents that morning.

■ Also in the area...

Ladybower and Derwent Reservoirs are just a few kilometres northeast. The 25km circuit of the two is exhilaratingly scenic, mostly traffic-free, and arguably the best reservoir cycle circuit in Britain. There are some long stretches of mildly rough offroad, not suitable for a thin-tyred racing bike, but OK for a decent tourer or hybrid. From Hope, head a couple of kilometres east on the main road, then left through Thornhill right up to the dam. Cross the dam top to the right hand side, turn left and follow the cycle path up the side of the reservoir. Turn left on the main road, and where the other reservoir splits off on the right, turn right to follow its eastern bank. This offroad path takes you right up to the top of the 10km-long pair of reservoirs; you cross a little bridge and come back down the quiet road on the other side. There's a visitor centre halfway. It's gently, gently uphill to the top

A625 was built to avoid; now it's the only way over. The surface is smooth, there are no sharp bends, and the line of sight is good. But there usually is fast traffic, and the road is pretty narrow. So just take it easy and enjoy a steady free ride and the momentous gorge scenery, which is almost rudely un-English. The road levels out and brings you effortlessly back to Castleton and through to Hope.

A rainy day is not a bad time to visit the slithering summit and its downwardly mobile lane. Mist and drizzle enhances the feeling of being in some far-flung part of the third world; you half-expect to find indigenous peasants huddled in tents, and irritatingly seen-it-all foreign backpackers telling you it was much better ten years ago. In Castleton or Hope there are plenty of agreeable places

the momentous gorge scenery is almost rudely un-English

of the reservoir, then steady, freewheely downhill all the way back. The World War II Dambusters practised here, in case you want to do any mock re-enactments.

For grittier stuff, the Peaks offer an unlimited number of ad hoc cycling trip opportunities, often with stunning views. Browsing OS maps, it's easy to string routes together from the hundreds of bridleways and surfaced lanes.

■ Other places like this

The east coast, from the Isle of Sheppey in Kent up through Norfolk to the plain of Holderness in East Yorkshire, is slipping away. The ginger-biscuit consistency of the cliffs, constantly being dunked in the swirling tea-coloured North Sea, munches the land away at rates of up to a metre a year in some places. As a consequence, many old lanes that used to lead somewhere now stop abruptly at the edge, sometimes blocked by flimsy barriers that will have to be brought back in a year or two anyway. If you're cycle-touring way off the beaten track in coastal East Yorkshire, explore Seaside Road in Aldbrough, where a housing estate and its service road system is disappearing over the cliff in almost monthly instalments (see www.eriding.net/media/coast.shtml). This area is said to be losing up to two metres a year in some places, one of the fastest disappearing coastlines in the world.

In East Anglia, Happisburgh (north-east of Norwich, and pronounced 'hazeboro'; see the website www.happisburgh.org.uk) is another coastal village being eaten away by the waves, with financially crippling results for the unfortunate land- and home-owners. Whatever is currently left of the Clifftop Road might be interesting to cycle along, although most of it should now be called Cliffbottom Road. Dunwich, in Suffolk, is another steadily-dissolving place where you'd be advised to rent rather than buy. It's also the endpoint of an annual cycle cult, the Dunwich Dynamo *(see page 102).*

Snackstop

Fish and chip shop, Castleton. *In centre of village, just south of main street, next to Youth Hostel. Cafes and tea rooms too.*

Quirkshop

Ye Olde Nag's Head, Castleton. *Old coaching inn in centre of village. Cask ales, food, good range of malt whiskies.*

Quirkshop

Sweaty after a hot day's riding? Hathersage, 5km east of Hope, has a heated outdoor hillside 33m swimming pool, open on summer weekdays. Float on your back and enjoy the curious sensation of being surrounded by Peak District scenery.

Tourer's tick list

✓ Ladybower Reservoir
✓ Visit some of the four caves
✓ Cycle Edale
✓ Panorama from Hollins Cross (1km bridleway from Mam Tor)

OS 110, grid ref SK132836
INFO Castleton Tourist Information, Buxton Road, Castleton, tel. 01433 620679

IRONBRIDGE

WHERE *Shropshire: Telford to Ironbridge (12km one way)*
WHAT *Traffic-free trail and riverside roads*
WHY *Historic iron bridge in picturesque Severn village*
HOW *Train to Telford*

This lovely, easy day ride, almost all of it car-free, takes you to the heartland of England's industrial revolution. Far from being a ravaged industrial wasteland, the Severn gorge is picturesque and quaint. At the end, you can cycle over a bridge that was the first of its type in the world, and which led indirectly to the early production of the bicycle itself.

An iron coathanger that started a revolution

Start from Telford station, and take the Silkin Way south, which follows an old railway line past plenty of interesting little sights. You can download a map of the route on www.telford.gov.uk. It takes you 9km to Coalport, on the Severn. Cross by the old bridge here to the south bank and turn right, following the riverside path 3km.

Here, on your right, a gate bars traffic from crossing over to a picture-postcard village – it's been closed to traffic since 1934, but you can cycle it. The crossing is a bridge made of iron, called the "Iron Bridge", and the village is Ironbridge. Thinking up new names evidently wasn't a preoccupation for those local Industrial Revolution pioneers Abraham Darby I (who pioneered the process of smelting iron ore with coke), Abraham Darby II (who devised a way to forge single iron beams), or Abraham Darby III (who made the bridge). Well, look how they named their children.

But we can forgive them not having a poet's way with words. (A poet such as Shropshire specialist AE Housman, for instance, always banging on about how the countryside's gone to the dogs and how we're all getting old and going to die). Because they were inventors, makers and doers. Right here, through the 1700s, the Abraham Darby dynasty refined ironmaking techniques around Coalbrookdale.

The Iron Bridge, opened on 1 Jan 1781, was a stunning example of what the new technology could do,

much admired by the world's visiting engineers. The village sprang up around it to house and feed the world's technical elite as they jotted their awed notes and diagrams. A new age of mass production took off, and that eventually included making bikes. Suddenly even the most modest wage-earner could afford a mode of transport that could take them wherever they pleased to go, for work or leisure.

The Iron Bridge is most impressive seen side-on, from the riverside path. It was vastly overengineered, built with twice as much iron as the load required, but it wasn't bad for a first shot. Two similar bridges

built shortly afterwards used less metal for more span. One was nearby at Buildwas, and is long gone. The second was at Coalport. A crossing had gone up in 1780 as a wooden bridge. But when Ironbridge was bolted into place the following year, Coalport's matchstick model must have looked so pre-industrial. So when it was rebuilt in 1810, they did it in the hip and trendy new material of iron. It's still standing, and taking traffic, today – it's the one you cycle over on the way here.

Its bigger brother at Ironbridge is only 30m across, so even with a few photo stops your trip here is unlikely to take up all of your afternoon. The pavement-cafe square by the bridge is charming, and the village has all that a modern cyclist needs; accommodation, a post office, restaurants, pubs, ice-cream parlour, pork-pie shop etc. It's a very English-scale experience, the sort of place that invites you to dawdle, take things easy, listen to Elgar and Vaughan Williams, and maybe write poems about how awful and unfair life is, before you retrace your steps to Telford.

a very English-scale experience

between comfortably, but going by car involves a lot of parking hassle. The enthusiastic tourist information office in Ironbridge village has plenty of maps and brochures.

National Cycle Route 45 will eventually connect Salisbury to Chester. It goes right past the south entrance to the Iron Bridge (in fact, you follow a short section of it in the route outlined above) and the stretch between there and Whitchurch is now open and signed. For the latest situation on the rest of it (south to Bridgnorth, Bewdley, Worcester, Gloucester etc) see Sustrans' web site (www.sustrans.org.uk).

From Telford, National Cycle Route 81 takes you east via Wolverhampton to Dudley, home of the monster tunnel at Netherton *(see page 114)* and on to Birmingham. After Wolverhampton it's almost all traffic-free on canal towpaths. Going west from Telford, Route 81 goes to Shrewsbury, and ultimately to Aberystwyth.

Another Sustrans route, the Six Castles Cycleway, largely follows quiet roads to links together Shrewsbury, Bishop's Castle, Ludlow and Leominster, with rail access at either end.

■ Also in the area

You can follow your nose round the gorge area and shuttle between the various attractions, which include several museums about the area's industrial history, and a bike is the ideal way to explore them. They're too far from each other to walk

■ Other places like this

Britain has quite a few historic bridges that were the first this or the most innovative that. The dra-

matic Clifton Suspension Bridge in Bristol, and the Menai over to Anglesey, are also historic and photogenic bridge crossings, for example. Both of them are shared with cars, though.

Clifton's vertiginous 200m crossing, 75m above the Avon gorge, was finished in 1864. Brunel's masterpiece is now a toll bridge for traffic but bikes still cross for free. On the one side is the smart suburb of Clifton, with its wine bars full of lawyers talking in loud voices, and on the other side is Ashton Court Estate. A pleasant, cyclable riverside path down below (part of the Avon Cycleway) follows the Avon gorge from Bristol's town centre docks, way out to Avonmouth.

The Menai suspension bridge is also mightily impressive. Built by Thomas Telford and completed in 1826, its 176m span was the first suspension bridge in the world. You cross it as part of the Lôn Las Cymru (Welsh National Cycle Route) which runs from Cardiff to Holyhead. It's a bit narrow,

though, and in busy traffic cyclists can feel unpleasantly hemmed in and hassled.

Gateshead's fabulous Millennium Bridge has made a little architectural history as the world's first tilting cycle bridge *(see page 174).*

Snackstop

Eley's Pork Pie Shop. *Gourmet pork pies and sausages right opposite the bridge.*

Bevvy break

The White Hart, Ironbridge. *Riverfront tables in a large, pleasant pub on the Wharfage, right by the bridge.*

Quirkshop

There's a remarkable natural phenomenon just outside Coalport: the Tar Tunnel (entrance £1.50), part of an old complex of old man-made tunnels and shafts that riddle the area. Its walls ooze with naturally-occurring tar (bitumen).

Tourer's tick list

✓ Industrial museums
✓ Severn gorge
✓ Bridgnorth
✓ Wenlock Edge

OS 127, grid ref SJ672033
INFO The Toll House, Ironbridge, Telford TF8 7AW, tel. 01952 432166, www.ironbridge.org.uk

Legendary Rosedale CHIMNEY BANK

CHIMNEY BANK

WHERE *Castleton, North Yorkshire: Circular ride via Rosedale Abbey (40km)*

WHAT *Strenuous but stunning ride in deepest North York Moors*

WHY *Convenient remoteness, and Britain's steepest road uphill*

HOW *Train to Castleton*

The North York Moors is an underrated gem for the cycle tourer who doesn't mind short, sharp, but gloriously scenic hills, and who enjoys friendly, convenient pubs and teashops and quaint villages. This route on narrow, lightly trafficked lanes offers great panoramas, as well as Britain's steepest uphill; Chimney Bank. (Harlech's Fford Pen Llech is steeper, but it's one way downhill!)

Britain's steepest uphill, in the North York Moors

Start from Castleton station, between Middlesbrough and Whitby. Head south, and up, towards Rosedale. After 7km you're at a panorama overlooking the shelf of the Moors, where you came from, and the vast bowl of Rosedale the other side. Take the left to Rosedale Abbey round the shoulder of the dale and hurtle downhill into the village of Rosedale Abbey. Immediately after the village take the right, by the Milburn Arms Hotel pub. There's an exciting sign for Chimney Bank: Gradient 1 in 3 Unsuitable for lorries (hip!), caravans (hip!) & coaches prohibited (hooray!). The warning is repeated, emphatically in red, further up.

This is your challenge for the day. Some hills, like wasps, seem to serve no function other than to cause pain. Cycle in certain parts of Devon, which swarms with pointless little stinging ascents, and you'll know what we mean. The North York Moors is also a hive of activity for makers of '1 in 3' road signs, but climbing efforts are richly rewarded. The bubble-wrap topography means that there's always a stiff little climb on a winding filament of tarmac out of the village or up from the main road; but minutes later, a wonderful, long, flat ridge crests the top of the moor. Enjoy sheepy solitude, the calls of curlews and snipes, not a man-made sight or sound. In late summer sun, the vast heather glows with potassium-permanganate purple; in the rain it hisses malevolently, and you're

another ghostly wisp in the stratus. Just as well that, despite the apparent isolation, you're only a five-minute swish down that tarmac chute to a postcard-perfect village with cottage teashop, pub, and chirpy local folks.

And here is Chimney Bank taking off from the village like a startled pheasant. Of the countless '1 in 3' signs gracing hills across England, this is the only genuine article, according to Guinness. It's an asphalt elevator that's about to whisk you to the Moors' top floor. It's tough, yes, but certainly rideable, and on a sunny day, glorious. With every metre of height gained, the gorgeous scenery below unfolds a little further.

There are three techniques for making an uphill hack go more quickly: (1) Guess how many pedal revolutions it will be to the top, and count down; (2) Swear copiously; (3) Get off and push.

There are several bends and hair-

pins, but it's not too long a slog - only 176m of climb. At Bank Top you cash in your investment. There's a bench on the left, a gravel car park on the right, and a sign warning downwards traffic to engage low gear, and cyclists to dismount. On an icy day, the descent's corners can arrange this automatically. This is the Spaunton Estate, and with a long gentle downhill, you can take things easy and enjoy the views, stopping often to take it in. A right at the junction leads down to Hutton-le-Hole, another sturdily beautiful village with pubs and greens, which could be the set for a 1920s period drama.

From here head back up north, along the other glorious side of Rosedale, past The Lion Inn at Blakey Top, to reach the panorama point you passed on the way out. From here it's downhill all the way back to Castleton.

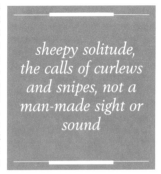

sheepy solitude, the calls of curlews and snipes, not a man-made sight or sound

■ Also in the area

The North York Moors is in our view the best part of the country for a certain type of cycle-touring - the type involving tea, pubs, friendly people, quaint villages, quirky stuff, a little effort and wonderful scenery. Spend a week in this compact marvel, never riding more than 20km from the centre, and you'll always feel like you're somewhere new. This is farm country: lasses on horses and lads on tractors, and 4x4s that have never been near a supermarket car park.

Instead of going north from Hutton-le-Hole, you can go south. It's downhill to the main road, which leads to Pickering another 9km or so away. There you can catch England's best train - see Grosmont and Pickering *(see page 162)*. Quite nearby is the surviving 'Roman Road surface' at Wheeldale Moor *(see page 118)* and, for a break from the hills, a flat rail trail runs along the coast from Scarborough to Whitby.

There are lots of well-gravelled off-road tracks which can be enjoyed on a sturdy road bike (as well as mountain bikes). Rudland Rigg, and the old railway track from Chimney Bank Top all the way up and round Rosedale and back to Rosedale Abbey, are pleasant rides and shouldn't be all that muddy.

■ Other places like this

Britain has plenty more big hill experiences on its rural roads. Porlock Hill, in Devon, is legendarily hard (2.2km of climb with two hairpins, reaching 25% in places). Everyone has a story about their granddad's Morris 8 having to go up in reverse.

Elsewhere in the county there are wall-of-death hills all over, many of them self-defeating. For instance, Millook Haven, about 7km south of Bude on the scribble of coastal minor-minor road, has a 1 in 3 descent on one side which is so steep and twisty you have to dismount and dig your heels in as you and bike lunge down, only for you to be instantly faced with a 1 in 3 up on the other side of the creek which you have to push laboriously up. You end up at the same height you started from.

Severe climbs don't come any more challenging than the snaking tarmac ribbons of Hardknott and Wrynose Passes in the Lake District, Hardknott being the nearest rival to Chimney Bank *(pictured below)*. It pitches, rolls and yaws its way through spectacular landscape between Eskdale and the Duddon Valley. Winding and full of narrow hairpins, this is surprisingly an old Roman Road, laid out in the 2nd century AD. The road was only surfaced after World War II, since it was obliterated by tank training. Honister Pass, near Buttermere in the Lake District, is another monster ascent with fabulous scenery and thundering downhills, with wide open views. Ride from Seatoller towards Buttermere.

Snackstop
Picnic. *On the green at Hutton-le-Hole. Or try the tea rooms at the Barn Hotel.*

Bevvy break
The Lion Inn, Blakey Top. *One of Britain's most remote pubs, 400m up on the highest point of the Moors. Great views, big range of cask beer, open fires. Worth a bike ride in itself.*

Quirkshop
This is sheep farming country, so you might well see sheepdogs in action, usually those beautiful black-and-white border collies. Those with odd-coloured eyes apparently mesmerise the sheep. Stop and enjoy the show.

Tourer's tick list
✓ Panorama from Rosedale Head
✓ Picnic lunch in moortop wilderness
✓ Village pubs, tea shops
✓ Get held up by sheep/cows
✓ Blazing purple heather from July to September

OS 94, grid ref SE725958
INFO Pickering Tourist Information Centre, The Ropery, Pickering, North Yorkshire YO18 8DY, tel. 01751 473791, www.pickering @ ytbtic.co.uk

Ferry, cross the Mersey, cause this land's the place I love

MERSEY FERRY

WHERE *Liverpool: Ferry terminal to New Brighton (12km return) or to Otterspool Promenade (16km return)*

WHAT *Flat car-free family-friendly promenade rides with seafront cityscapes*

WHY *The famous, friendly Mersey Ferry*

HOW *Train to Liverpool Lime St*

Do either, or both, of these easy, flat promenade rides suitable for all the family - but make sure you take your bike on the legendary Mersey Ferry, a unique experience for cyclists that's so characteristic of the City of Culture.

The famous Liverpool water shuttle

From Liverpool Lime St, head west a kilometre to the ferry terminal. Ride 1 heads south 8km all along the waterfront to Otterspool Promenade, passing Albert Dock. Said to be the biggest collection of Grade 1 listed buildings in Britain, the complex includes swish shops and bars, as well as Tate Liverpool and the Beatles Story. At the end, either retrace your steps, or come back by train from Cressington Station a few metres inland, to return to the ferry terminal.

It's very nice too. But Ride 2 is better: you actually take the ferry, across to Seacombe in Birkenhead. They say it's "the world's most famous ferry", and with a collection of popular cultural references behind it, it's hard to disagree with. Did Gerry and the Pacemakers have a hit in 1965 with Ferry 'Cross the Humber? Did the chart-topping charity followup by a consortium of Liverpool artists in 1989 celebrate the Harwich-Felixstowe crossing? Was there a 1960s electric guitar-based popular-music style called the Woolwich Beat?

The ferry shuttles a triangular course. Liverpool's Pier Head is the eastern apex. Across the water on the Wirral, Woodside is at the southern apex, and Seacombe on the northern. From there you head back to Pier Head. It is, of course, pedestrians and cyclists only: motor traffic takes the tunnel. That personal scale is largely what makes its charm.

The ticket office is 400m from Pier Head, so a bike is useful if you're rushing to make a departure. Services are half-hourly at commuting times, hourly outside, and run from about 7.30am-7pm. Tickets are a very reasonable £1.35 single, £2.15 return, and bikes are free.

The ferry itself is a proper working shuttle-sized boat, not a sugary tourist experience. There are no souvenir stalls on board or public address systems playing 1960s singles interspersed with faux DJ-speak, at least, there weren't on our trip. Thank goodness. You get a fine view of the iconic trio of waterfront buildings - the Royal Liver, with statues of the mythical liver birds on top; the Cunard; the Port of Liverpool - which you can photograph at leisure if you come outside the rush hours, when you will most probably have the boat to yourself.

For the best experience though, come at peak times. In the morning, there will be 10-20 cyclists and uncountable pedestrians on each Liverpool-bound service, and a sim-

back to the terminal for the return ferry to Liverpool.

■ Also in the area

Cyclists can get the best out of the area round the three ferry terminals. At Woodside - gateway to Birkenhead - maybe get off and pop in to Hamilton Square, the expansive public space just up behind the red-brick clock tower seen from the terminal buildings. Then take the next ferry (or cycle - it's only 3km or so) to Seacombe.

ilar number going back in the evening.

Each crossing is only ten minutes or so, but that's plenty of time for a natter and a bit of a laugh. Like cyclists the world over they're a chatty lot here, friendly and open, but with that extra topping of Scouse wit. (When I took a snap of a couple of lads, saying I wanted the Liver Building in the background, the flash went off. "Must be a powerful flash," one quipped, "if it can light up the Liver Buildin' from 'ere." OK, so that's not Oscar Wilde standard maybe, but you never saw him on a bike in Toxteth.)

At Seacombe you can get off the ferry and immediately cycle 7km on the traffic-free waterside path up to New Brighton. The views aren't chocolate-box twee, but there's a breezy thrill in the expansive docks, cranes, wind turbines and purpose-ful water traffic. Retrace your steps

Liverpool has plenty of ways to keep you entertained in between ferry trips. Architecturally it's impressive, but cycling round the centre in busy traffic to see it might not be too relaxing. The Anglican Cathedral, to the south-east, is impressive too; the Metropolitan Cathedral is also worth a look. Walker Art Gallery is near the station.

For the best experience, come at peak times

Instead of turning back at New Brighton, you can continue along the waterfront, still traffic-free, for another few kilometres. From here the route continues, as National Cycle Route 56, to Chester.

Liverpool is on the unsung Trans-Pennine Trail (National Cycle Routes 62 and 65), a 350km route that runs coast-to-coast from Southport across to Hornsea, east of Hull. Most of the route is off-road, using canals and rail trails and so on, and so it's surprisingly light on hills. It makes a fine tour of five to seven days; do it westwards to have the wind mostly behind you.

■ Other places like this

A car-free, big-river ferry, with a subculture, in a major city... Mersey's celebrated shuttle is pretty much unique. The Thames has some carless ferries that you can take your bike onto (see www.tfl.gov.uk/river), and some of the eastside ones are lots of fun (London Bridge to Masthouse, for instance). They're intended for commuters and getting a bike on may be a question of squeezing it between seats. But there are so many convenient (and cheaper, or free) alternative ways to get you and your bike across or up the water, the boats somehow don't have the same feel of common purpose. Woolwich's free ferry, out east on the Thames, is an atmos-

pheric must-do *(see page 62)* though of course it takes cars and lorries.

Gosport in Hampshire may be the nearest to a 'southern Mersey ferry' *(see page 154)*. A passenger and cycle ferry running all day 363 days a year, it's particularly useful to cyclists because it saves the 20km-plus road alternative round Portsmouth harbour (which motorists have to do). The Harwich-Felixstowe crossing *(see page 98)* is also something special, but in terms of branding neither can quite match the Mersey. We're not aware of any Gosport musical legends, or major chart hits by a Harwich-based beat combo.

Snackstop

Dockside. *There's any number of cafes in the Albert Dock and city centre, but if the weather's decent enough to sit outside, stock up from the shops and picnic on the front over at Woodside, with a view of the Liverpool skyline.*

Bevvy break

Pumphouse, Dockside. *Average, touristy sort of pub a kilometre or so south of the ferry; you can sit outside in a smallish beer "garden".*

Quirkshop

Beatles fans can make a cycle pilgrimage with maps and brochures from the tourist office. Penny Lane is 9km-10km from the ferry terminal: head 5km south along the promenade, then north/east on the Sefton Park cycle route.

Tourer's tick list

✓ Art galleries
✓ Grand architecture
✓ Albert Dock area
✓ Cathedrals
✓ Beatles pilgrimage

OS 108, grid ref Sj338902
INFO Mersey Ferries
tel. 0151 3301444,
info@merseyferries.co.uk; Liverpool
Tourist Information, Queen Square,
Liverpool L1 1RG,
askme@visitliverpool.com

THE HUMBER BRIDGE

HUMBER BRIDGE

WHERE *North Ferriby, East Yorkshire to South Ferriby, Lincolnshire (12km one way)*

WHAT *Flat car-free shore ride by River Humber*

WHY *Longest cyclable single-span bridge in world*

HOW *Train to North Ferriby*

This flat, photogenic offroad ride - easy for mountain bikes, doable on a sturdy touring bike or hybrid - takes you between two namesake but very separate villages via one of the world's great cycling experiences: a crossing of the Humber Bridge.

Still the world's best suspension bridge for cyclists

Start from North Ferriby station (which is just called 'Ferriby'). Head towards the village church and turn right. Just after the railway bridge turn left into the discreetly signed riverside park. You get a splendid side-on view of the bridge from here. Follow the riverside path to the bridge. It's a bit bumpy. Go underneath the bridge on the river-front lane and follow cycle signs to the Bridge; it's a cumbersome route, and you can short-cut it by going left before the bridge if you don't mind humping your bike up steps and through gates.

The Humber Bridge is a mightily impressive structure. When it opened in 1981, it was the longest single-span suspension bridge in the world, with towers 1410m apart. Today it's only fourth in the main-span league table, overtaken by more ambitious upstarts, but if you turn up on a bike, hoping to cross the Akashi-Kaikyo in Japan (1991m), the Great Belt in Denmark (1624m), or the Runyang in China (1490m), you'll be disappointed. And not allowed across. They have no cycle lanes or footways.

So hooray for the Humber Bridge! The estuary may be the sort of brown usually found on stray dogs; the most vertical points on the surrounding scenery may be the distant hazy smokestacks of Grimsby and Immingham; and it may only join Hull, a city of 300,000 people, with some fields on the other side, but it does welcome cyclists and walkers, as a proper bridge should.

And cycling is the ideal way to enjoy the world's fourth-longest - and still best - single-span suspension bridge. In a car you can't stop to admire the engineering; on foot it's just too far across, but bike pace is just right. Feel the awesome scale and precarious windswept isolation in the middle, just a few minutes away from coffee and cake.

Here on the north side, there's a large car park, cafe, information centre and viewing area right next to the tower. You go through it to get to the bridge's cycle lane (both sides have one but only the eastside one is usually open these days). The path is wide, smooth, and over-looked by the rocket-launcher towers and massively graceful cables. It's not as far as it looks down to the ships below (only 30m), but the mildly choppy waters are deceptive. The Humber is said to be the world's most dangerous river for shipping after the Orinoco - not from pirates, piranhas or crocs, but the shifting sandbars which demand expert local knowledge from the Humber Pilots.

The north tower is solidly on land; the south tower is out in the estuary, whose mud-pie geology put the building years behind schedule in the 1970s as every concrete support they put in place disappeared. The best place to photograph the bridge as a structure is from the south bank, thanks to the graceful curve on the approach road.

Landing in Barton (which has a remote railway station), double back towards the foreshore and turn

or take a train from Hessle, whose station is just by the north tower.

■ Also in the area

The Humber Bridge is on the White Rose Route, which goes 200km from Hull to Middlesbrough *(see page 158)*, passing some quietly delightful villages such as Ferriby and Welton. You may be surprised by the well-to-do Sussex-Downs feel of these villages.

Going east from the Bridge, you can, with persistence, stay next to the water all the way through docklands to the centre of Hull; or follow the Sustrans Route 1 signs from the Bridge to Hull through Hessle, along roads and paths.

You can easily cycle traffic-free along the waterfront from Hull Marina, round the world's biggest fishtank, the brilliant *The Deep* and beyond, with sweeping industrial views, to the dockside departure point for North Sea Ferries (about 13km from the bridge). These boats offer a comfortable and inexpensive glide overnight, either to Rotterdam or to Zeebrugge, which is just an hour's ride away from Bruges.

left to go west along the riverside path. That takes you to the village of South Ferriby where you can look back across the water to North Ferriby and see your entire route. Before the bridge opened, these communities had nothing whatever to do with each other except the name: they were different counties, separated totally by the river, looking across at each other as if in different countries. Since the bridge opened, they have had nothing whatever to do with each other either.

Retrace your steps back to Ferriby;

The most dangerous shipping lane after the Orinoco

National Cycle Route 1, from Dover to John O'Groats, goes over the Humber Bridge.

National Cycle Route 65 (the last leg of the Trans Pennine Trail) goes from Hull centre along a flat, unspectacular railtrail to the modest seaside town of Hornsea 22km away. Or get your kicks on Route 66 from Hull along another flat trail to another modest seaside resort, Withernsea. Going west from Hull, you can take the Trans Pennine Trail all the way to Liverpool *(see Mersey Ferry entry on page 154)*.

■ Other places like this

The Severn Bridge crossing is very similar in atmosphere, setting, and in how long it feels, although its main span is quite a bit shorter at 990m. In fact, the Humber's design was modelled closely on the Severn's graceful suspended arch. Surprisingly, the Severn Bridge begins and ends in England - it continues west across a further cable-stayed bridge over the River Wye, which is the crossing-point into Wales, giving an impression of greater overall length. From the bridge is a splendid view of the Second Severn crossing just to the south, which like all too many bridges of recent times has no provision for bikes. The Severn Bridge also has a cycle-cum-pedestrian lane either side and, because it carries the M48, it offers the chance possibly unique in the UK to 'cycle on a motorway' - well, sort of. Right alongside a motorway, anyway. The experience is most potent on the Wye Bridge section, where the cycle lane is just a few feet from the motorway traffic. The south-side bike path passes a large blue motorway direction sign, by which you could photograph youself. There is also the curious experience of cycling to a motorway service area: Severn View Services are immediately east of the Bridge.

The Tamar Bridge, links Devon and Cornwall, and has recently had a separate pedestrian-cycle lane added. Though only a quarter the length of the Humber Bridge, it's still a very impressive and atmospheric crossing.

Snackstop
Reading Room Cafe, Low St, North Ferriby. *Excellent, cosy little place, with newspapers, good coffee and quality food, tucked away in a back lane; ask for directions!*

Bevvy break
Duke of Cumberland, Ferriby. *Grand old pub on the old main road with outside tables.*

Quirkshop
Over the bridge and on the south bank, 2km south and 1km west of South Ferriby, is the riddle of Horkstow Bridge - a splendid miniature 19th-century suspension bridge, a few metres long, going from nowhere to nowhere for no apparent reason, over a drain. Like the Humber Bridge, then, but smaller.

Tourer's tick list
✓ Villages: Ferriby, Swanland, Welton
✓ Side view of bridge from north foreshore
✓ Straight-on view of bridge from south foreshore
✓ Docky, industrial foreshore
✓ The Deep, Hull Marina

OS 106, grid ref TA 026245
INFO Humber Bridge Tourist Information Centre, Ferriby Road, Hessle, East Yorkshire HU13 0JG, tel. 01482 640852, humber-bridge.tic @ eastriding.gov.uk

NORTH YORK MOORS

WHERE   *Whitby, North Yorkshire: Circular ride (50km)*

WHAT   *Britain's best day ride: moors, forest, coasts; trains, lanes, rail trails*

WHY   *Wonderful scenery, and England's most atmospheric train ride*

HOW   *Train to Whitby*

This is the all-day ride with everything: moortop exhilaration; forest beauty; coastal sweeps; characterful towns; a mighty aqueduct; sparsely-trafficked country lanes; car-free rail trails; England's best fish and chips; and a time-travel train, the North York Moors Railway, that transports you and bike back to a gentler and politer age.

Time-travel on the lovely North York Moors Railway

Start early as possible from Whitby, taking your bike on the mainline train along the Esk valley to Grosmont. (Or cycle it; it's pleasant and flattish, but adds 12km to an already long day.) At Grosmont station, move across the platform to another train - an another era. The North Yorkshire Moors Railway (NYMR, www.nymr.co.uk) is a 1950s sort of place, in the best way. Trains chug between Grosmont and Pickering, chuffing a haze of steam over flat-capped farmers in green ties and Morris 1000s, tin boards advertising Woodbines, hoodless teenagers politely holding village shop doors open for ladies in hats, trains arriving on time, and smiling porters. The villages and hills are much the same, the beer just as refreshing. On a 1950s bike with cycle clips, a bottle of brown ale and a pork pie in the saddlebag, the time-warp experience will be complete. No wonder so many nostalgic TV dramas - All Creatures Great and Small, Heartbeat - have been set around here.

The NYMR is only one of many heritage railways in England, but it's a leading candidate for the best. It runs several trains a day, puffing through fabulous scenery, stopping at excellently-preserved stations, with sturdy, steam-period rolling stock, and all staffed by friendly locals who act as if they have the best unpaid job in the world. Bikes are welcome and go in an old-style cavernous guard's van.

Leave yourself at least a good half hour to poke around the village and explore the station before the train leaves, although with hourly services in summer, there's never too long a wait. If you do have a wait, the station has a tearoom. Tickets are not cheap (about £12 single to Pickering, plus £2 for bike) but, honestly, it's worth it. At the Grosmont end, the tickets issued are the old-style rectangles of card. Quite substantial enough to prop up a wonky tearoom table.

The ride to Pickering winds for an hour through the lovely Yorkshire scenery. Take the time to enjoy a cup of tea from the buffet, and take heed of the Hydra-like warning over the chunky old slam-doors that warns: *IT IS DANGEROUS FOR PAS-*

ulous car-free coastal views lead to Whitby, all level or long and gentle downhill on decent cinder track. North of Scarborough the rail trail doesn't offer a great deal to see for the next few miles, until the scenery suddenly unfolds when you get to Stoupe Brow, past Ravenscar.

A little further on, Robin Hood's Bay resembles a raked Cornish fishing village transplanted to the east coast, and is a good place to stop for a cuppa. A dramatic viaduct brings you high over the Esk back into Whitby.

SENGERS TO PUT THEIR HEADS OUT OF THE CARRIAGE WINDOWS.

Pickering is a bustling moors town with a solid, functioning feel, and one of those old-style electrical shops in the high street, displaying one of everything in the window with prices on fluorescent card. Head east on the main A170 4km to Thornton-le-Dale, a postcard-perfect village. Head north up the minor road at the crossroads and at the top of the hill take the right, to Dalby Forest Drive (free for bikes). The delightful forestry-commission ride leads you to quaint Hackness and the Forge Valley. Head east to Burniston, just north of Scarborough, and ask a friendly local where you can pick up the Scarborough-Whitby rail trail. This thankfully underrated gem is one of the country's most thrilling. (It's about 25km from Pickering to the rail trail.) From here, another 30km or so of fab-

■ Also in the area

If you want to dawdle, get a day rover ticket on the NYMR train and go down to Pickering in instalments. Get off at intermediate stations and cycle straight into wonderful, remote countryside. All the North York Moors area is wonderful for cycling, a compact, beautiful and underrated gem worth spending a few days on - but it can be very hilly *(see Chimney Bank on page 150).*

West of Pickering, in the south-west of the Moors, the Rye valley out of Helmsley is a good place for cycling exploration, and on the south-western tip of Moors, on Sutton Bank, a white horse is cut into the hillside *(for more white horses, see Caen Hill, page 30).* A narrow, very steep lane leads right past it from Kilburn.

30km or so of fabulous car-free coastal views

The Scarborough-Whitby rail trail is part of Sustrans' National Cycle Route 1, which goes from Dover to John O'Groats up the eastern side of England. Coming from the south, Route 1 will take you mainly along roads from the Humber Bridge *(see page 158)* through Hull up to Scarborough. Beyond Whitby, Route 1 takes you on a mixture of roads and tracks to Middlesborough, which is at the northern end of the White Rose Route (NCN 65) - which, to complete a giant week-long loop round east and north-east Yorkshire, can take you back to Hull via York.

■ Other places like this

England has plenty of heritage railways, most very accommodating to cyclists thanks to their roomy guard's vans: Wikipedia lists 70 standard gauge, 40 narrow gauge and 24 miniature, so there will be one near enough, and suitable for inclusion in almost any cycling time-tour. Here are some favourites of ours:

Severn Valley: Kidderminster-Bridgnorth, www.svr.co.uk *(see also Ironbridge on page 146)*.
West Somerset: Bishop's Lydeard-Minehead, www.west-somerset-railway.co.uk.
Keighley & Worth Valley: Keighley-Oxenhope, www.kwvr.co.uk *(see page 33)*.
Llangollen: Llangollen-Carrog, www.llangollen-railway.co.uk *(see page 132)*.
Paignton & Dartmouth: Paignton-Kingswear, www.paignton-steamrailway.co.uk.
Bluebell: Kingscote-Sheffield Park, www.bluebell-railway.co.uk.

Also, see the ride around the railway at Romney, Hythe & Dymchurch *(page 50)*.

For another scenic rail trail, see the entry on Staple Hill *(page 22)*. For shady forest riding, see Blackpool Bridge *(page 118)*.

Snackstop
Magpie Cafe, Whitby. *Candidate for Britain's best fish and chips, at normal prices, in this harbourfront cafe. Just look for the mammoth queue of backpackers.*

Bevvy break
White Swan Inn, Market Place, Pickering. *Snug evening choice. Station Tavern in Grosmont has outside tables.*

Quirkshop
Complete your time-travel experience with a trip to a more sedate age of motoring. In pretty Thornton-le-Dale, east of Pickering, is a delightful vintage car museum in Roxby Garage (www.nymm.co.uk). There are 40-odd cars and 30-odd bikes from the 1920s onwards.

Tourer's tick list
✓ Thornton-le-Dale
✓ Dalby Forest
✓ Robin Hood's Bay
✓ Whitby
✓ Purple heather in summer/autumn

OS 94, grid ref NZ828053
INFO Pickering Tourist Information Centre, The Ropery, Pickering, North Yorkshire YO18 8DY, tel. 01751 473791, www.pickering @ ytbtic.co.uk; timetables northyorkshiremoorsrailways.com, 01751 473535, contact 01751 427508

YORK PLANETS

WHERE *North Yorkshire: Selby to York (24km)*

WHAT *Flat family-friendly car-free rail trail*

WHY *Ride the solar system from Pluto to the sun*

HOW *Train to Selby, train back from York*

This easy, mostly car-free day ride, and ending in the bike-friendly tourist gem of York, won't win any prizes for scenery. It rumbles through unremarkable flat landscapes. But it has something astronomically better: a 1:575,872,239 scale model of the solar system, with planets sized and positioned by York University (www.solar.york.ac.uk). Which makes it the world's longest cycle path, at 6 billion kilometres.

A six-billion-kilometre cycle-path, all the way to Pluto

Start from Selby station and head a few metres east over the river to join National Cycle Route 65. It takes you alongside the River Ouse for a kilometre, then side roads and paths for about 7km. Just after the village of Riccall you join the long straight stretch of old railway that will take you to York - and right through all the planets. For on your right, on a hillock, is a tiny 6mm sphere, mounted on a post and with explanatory plaques. This is Pluto, and its minuscule size (the next planet is nowhere in sight) starts to give you a vivid feel for the emptiness of space. (Now it's officially '134340 Pluto', following its relegation in August 2006 to the minor league of planets along with other distant orbital chaff such as 90377 Sedna, 136199 Eris, and 50000 Quaoar.) Charon, Pluto's satellite twin, is here too.

Two and a bit kilometres further on comes orange-sized Neptune; 3km beyond that and about as big, Uranus, and the path's surface changes from unmade chalky ground to tarmac. It's another two and a bit kilometres to Saturn, rings and all - you can see how lonely these outer planets are, very different from the crowded celestial pool table suggested by the old school textbooks.

But things are beginning to get crowded. Only a kilometre beyond, outside a housing estate, is football-sized Jupiter, painted with swirly red bands just like the real stormy gas giant. Strictly speaking,

the next kilometre should be swarming with asteroids, those astronomical troublemakers that may or may not collide with earth one day soon. In fact, you pass through a housing development at Bishopthorpe, where children kick Jupiter-sized footballs.

Immediately after, it's all so hectic. There's Mars, a vivid crimson pea; 136m later is the Earth, a blue and green cherry tomato adorned with continents and oceans and the Moon; 72m past that is boiling Venus; 87m beyond, the sun-scorched ball-bearing of Mercury. And suddenly, 101m past that at a bike path junction, is the giant yellow sun: 2.4m in diameter, and a whole 10.3km from isolated Pluto. But if Pluto seems remote, consider that on this scale our nearest stellar neighbours - the Alpha Centauri family - would be 70,000km away.

muters, locals and leisure riders will be sharing the solar system with you. Your chances of being hit by one of them are much greater.

Also in the area

York is a delight to explore by bike. Its attractions, such as the city walls, Minster, twee medieval lane The Shambles, Yorkshire Wheel, riverside and splendid railway museum, are less than 4km from the sun. If you have an hour or two to spare before your train home, cycle up and down the riverside path by the Ouse.

In airmiles that distance would get you right round the world and still have enough left to go to Hawaii. Space is comprised of an awful lot of not very much.

Follow the signs right at the sun, through the racecourse and past Terry's (now Suchard's) chocolate factory. You go over the Ouse on the elegant new Millennium Bridge in Fulford, a pedestrian- and cycle-only traverse that looks like a space giant's harp, and along the river into York centre. Curiously (given the conversion of that old Selby-York line into the railtrail) trains still run direct from York station back to Selby.

But why not stay? York is one of England's top cycling cities, so as you stop to take pictures of yourself pondering the improbability of an asteroid contriving to collide with us in such an attenuated universe, you're unlikely to be alone. A steady trickle of com-

The cycle path from York to Selby is part of Sustrans' White Rose route, aka National Cycle Route 65, which runs 200km from Hull up to Middlesbrough. It can be ridden in two to three days: the first, from Hull to York is generally flat and tranquil, with views of the Humber estuary *(see the Humber Bridge entry on page 158)* followed by the planet parade. After York are one or two days of delightful North York Moors scenery: Byland Abbey, the White Horse, ridgetop riding, and Cod Beck Reservoir among the highlights. Hawnby is a likely place to stay.

Selby is on the Trans Pennine Route, which runs 350km from Southport to Hornsea via Liverpool and Hull. It's miraculously traffic-free for much of its length.

York is on National Cycle Route

a bridge that looks like a space giant's harp

66, from Beverley (a little north of Hull) to Manchester via Leeds. The route is open and signed between Beverley and York, and along the Leeds to Shipley Canal.

■ Other places like this

There's another Sustrans route that similarly compresses the solar system, on the canal between Taunton and Bridgwater. In this case the sun is halfway between them, at Maunsel Lock (OS 193, grid ref ST309298) and a double set of planets ranges out from the sun in each direction. It's 23km along the canal from the Bridgwater Pluto (OS 182, grid ref ST294366) to the Taunton Pluto (OS 193, grid ref ST239259), which is in a supermarket car park. For more information on the planets route, call 01823 330665.

Summer to spare? Jodrell Bank, in Cheshire, is overseeing an even larger scale (1 in 15 million) planetary modelling project over the whole of the UK (see the website www.spacedout-uk.com/solar_system). The huge stripey sun is at Jodrell Bank. The Earth is already in Macclesfield, Neptune is scheduled for Armagh and Pluto will be in Aberdeen. The project includes asteroids, comets and so on, too.

Another scale-bending artwork, this time expanding the microscopic to the enormous, is in Cambridge (OS154, grid ref TL459542). A kilometre or so of Cycle Route 11, out from the city's Addenbrooke's Hospital parallel to the railway near Great Shelford, has been covered in over 10,000 multicoloured stripes *(pictured, left)*. Each stripe represents one of the four letters in the human gene BRCA2, which was sequenced in Cambridge. This installation also celebrates the 10,000th mile of the National Cycle Network, whose 'precise' point is at an otherwise unmarked metal frame a few metres further past the end of the stripey section.

Snackstop
Betty's, St Helen's Square. *York's cream tea institution.*

Bevvy break
Kings Arms, riverside by Ouse Bridge, York. *Outdoor waterside tables at famously flooding pub - inexpensive beer but shame about the unpleasant service on our visit.*

Quirkshop
According to the Ghost Research Foundation International, York is the most haunted city in the world, with 504 hauntings. Ghost walks (Kings Arms, 8pm) but no ghost cycle ride. York ghosts are usually indoors (Roman soldiers in Treasurer's House cellars, Catherine Howard in the King's Manor); but if you cycle up and down the riverside path on a lonely, foggy night you might find Ghost No. 505.

Tourer's tick list
- ✓ York (Minster, rail museum, Jorvik Museum, Shambles etc)
- ✓ Cycle round and through its city walls
- ✓ Millennium Bridge
- ✓ Picture your bike wheel against Yorkshire Wheel from towpath

OS 105, grid ref SE582482
INFO York Tourist Information, Railway Station, York YO24 1AY, tel. 01904 550099, tourism@yorkvic.co.uk, www.solar.york.ac.uk

"*it's all downhill to* *Dentdale*"

DENTDALE

WHERE *Dentdale, North Yorkshire: Circular ride via Dent (40km)*

WHAT *Hilly country lanes in fabulous Dales scenery*

WHY *Best long downhill in Britain?*

HOW *Train to Dent station*

This strenuous, but very rewarding, day ride takes you through wonderful Dales scenery, finishing on one of England's longest, and arguably most enjoyable, long downhills, ending in an essential Dales town.

Perhaps the country's most enjoyable scenic freewheel

Start from Dent station (the highest mainline station in England, on the gloriously scenic and famous Carlisle-Settle line). A very steep downhill takes you to Cowgill; turn right for Dent, and shortly after switch over to the opposite bank of the little river on the lane that runs parallel. Just before Dent, turn left up a steep lane to Ingleton. About 10km later (7km of which is uphill) is Yorda's Cave (SD705791) on your right. It's well worth investigating, with a non-touristy, 'real' feel thanks to having no information boards or signs. Come with a torch, sticking-plaster and TCP. You're in for a treat: you'll feel that you've discovered it by yourself.

From Ingleton (which has an outdoor heated swimming pool - www.ingletonpool.co.uk) head out north-east on the tiny lane parallel to the B6255. Eventually it joins that B road. On the B6255, just beyond Ribblehead Station, turn left off the main road just after the pub on the chalky track. It leads immediately under the awesome Ribblehead Viaduct, with its 24 arches spanning 400m. It's not the country's longest (Harrington aka Welland viaduct, just south of Rutland Water, has 82 arches and is over 1200m, and a minor road goes under one of its arches) but it's a dramatic component of the landscape, and if you're lucky you'll see a train on the Settle-Carlisle run chugging across it. Turn round and go back to the B6255.

About 6km-7km after Ribblehead,

on Blea Moor, turn left down the narrow lane to Dent. After a short stretch of moory rooftop, the way suddenly dips down in front of you, under a railway viaduct, with splendid Dales hills as a background. From here, you can forget all about pedalling. The first few hundred metres are steep and twisty, but shortly after going under the viaduct is the gentle slope that will propel you into Dent: your immense downhill reward for all that climbing earlier on.

It's only about 5km-7km of guaranteed freewheel, though a fresh easterly can add one or two more. There are certainly longer freewheels elsewhere; the A road plunging down from Hartside to Alston in Cumbria, for example, might give you 9km for free, depending on wind, for instance. But you can't relax doing it - it's a busy A road -

engineers who decided to put the station so far up.

and you see little scenery. So for all-round, easy, unfolding pleasantness, this descent into Dent is hard to beat. From a windswept moortop into gorgeous green dale, and ending up at a cobbled Dales village. It's very lightly trafficked, and for most of its length it's very, very gradual downhill - just enough to keep momentum, but not so steep that trivia such as braking or steering will impinge on the enjoyment of the scenery.

Scooting gently along, there's just enough momentum to hop over a couple of pocket-sized bridges as the dales develop on all sides. You pass a junction you saw this morning: this time, stick to the right hand side of the river. With a strong tailwind you might just freewheel all 10km or so to Dent, the perfect Dales village for cyclists. It has quaint cobbled streets, pubs, teashops and a campsite right in the town centre. It's also a real, living place, and an ideal base for cycling the extraordinary surroundings.

To get back to the station from Dent, you have to head back east along the valley - and curse the

Dent, the perfect Dales village for cyclists

◼ Also in the area

All around the Yorkshire Dales are innumerable cycling opportunities, and many of them are wonderful (www.cyclethedales.org.uk/routes). Any narrow yellow thread on the OS map is fun for exploring. The Dee valley north-east out of Dent, for instance, is lovely stuff, while any excursions round the areas of Wharfedale, Littondale or Malham will be tiring but exhilarating.

The Yorkshire Dales Cycleway is a signed, 210km circuit that takes you through most of the major dales; it also passes through Dent. The YDC makes for a challenging but enormously satisfying tour of 4-7 days. The six sections, each 35km-40km, start and end in Skipton - Malham - Ingleton - Hawes - Grinton - Kettlewell - Skipton. It's possible to get your luggage transported between destinations by a special van delivery service (www.sherpavan.com).

Another day ride from Dent can take you to Cam High Road, the country's most exciting Roman road *(see page 182)*. You're also not that far from the Great Dun Fell road, the highest cyclable road in Britain *(see page 186)*.

Dent is right on the Pennine Cycleway (Sustrans National Cycle

Route 68; nothing to do with the Pennine Way or Pennine Bridleway). This very long distance path runs 580km up the spine of England from Derby to Berwick. The Dales portion of the route runs through Settle – Clapham – Ingleton – Dent – Sedbergh – Kirkby Stephen.

National Cycle Route 7 goes from Carlisle to Inverness; one day National Cycle Route 69 is planned to connect Morecambe with Selby via Settle.

■ Other places like this

England's longest cyclable downhill for mountain bikers is probably the slingshot track down from the summit of Skiddaw: in just 7km the rough bridleway falls over 800m. Long road freewheels include a 5km-7km stretch from Allenheads to Rookhope in the Pennines. Like the Hartside-Alston downhill mentioned above, it's on the fantastic Sustrans Sea to Sea (C2C) route, but is on a main road.

However, the last leg of the C2C – the one that takes you to the east coast – offers what may be the longest assisted cycle in England, given the right weather. It runs down the Waskerley Way, which is gently downhill all the way from the Pennines into Sunderland. The overwhelming prevailing wind is right behind you, enabling you to pedal very easily for around 20km; in really strong tailwinds you may be able to freewheel much of that. (the route was designed with this effect in mind.) It's the nearest you'll get to a cycling perpetual motion machine. The hour-long moving walkway starts just after your final ascent of the trip, out from Rookhope *(pictured left)*. Then you're on the old railway line that rolls exhilaratingly down – it feels like all the way – to the sea at Newcastle or Sunderland, for one of the most satisfying hour's cycling of your whole life.

Snackstop
Stone Close Tea Room, Dent. *Classy 17th-century cottage cafe and snackery with flagstone floors and iron ranges, right in heart of the village, on the cobbled 'main street'.*

Bevvy break
Sun Inn, Dent. *Fabulous traditional Dales pub, another historic (16th-century) building on cobbled main street; brews its own beer.*

Quirkshop
Visit the Sun Inn and sample a genuine, local-brewed beer. Dent Brewery was formed behind the pub to sell beer only in the pub itself, but their ales became so popular they expanded and moved up the valley to Cowgill. It's now on sale across England, even in a House of Commons bar!

Tourer's tick list
✓ Ribblehead viaduct
✓ Yorda's Cave
✓ Ingleton
✓ Stay in Dent
✓ Settle–Carlisle railway

OS 98, grid ref SD783839
INFO Ingleton Tourist Information, Community Centre Car Park, Main St, Ingleton, Carnforth LA6 3HJ, tel. 015242 41049 (open daily Apr–Sep)

TYNE TUNNEL & GATESHEAD

WHERE *Newcastle: Gateshead to Jarrow and back (24km return)*

WHAT *Flat urban riverside ride on paths and roads*

WHY *Town riverscape, Millennium Bridge, Tyne Tunnel*

HOW *Train to Newcastle*

This easy day ride showcases Newcastle's lively town centre, with two thrilling cycle-only crossings of the Tyne: from the unique Millennium Bridge to the weird Tyne Tunnel.

Newcastle's great tiled drainpipe under the Tyne

Newcastle's train station is on the north bank, so head out the station south to the riverside path. It's a Sustrans route, one of the alternative endings of their Coast to Coast routes (C2C). Several impressive bridges crowd together to cross the river like a forest canopy, including the famous lofty steel coathanger (which has a bike lane). But we're heading east, so turn left and head a few hundred metres downriver along the bustling path to the elegant suspended horseshoe of the Gateshead Millennium Bridge. The entire structure can tilt up and back like an opening eyelid, to allow shipping to pass underneath, and its elegant simplicity won it the prestigious Stirling Prize in 2002.

Best of all, Gateshead's iconic facility was designed purposely with the cyclist in mind. The inner arc is a pedestrian-only path, the outer for cyclists and walkers. Cross over on it. On the other side, shackle your bike and explore the Baltic Mills building, now a snazzy Tate-Modern-style art space with a combination of free and paid-for exhibitions, plus a cafe and shop. Up on the top floor is a viewing area with a splendid bird's-eye view of the bridge and of its colleagues.

Carry on along the south bank. A signed cycle path takes you on paths and the odd back road 11km or so to Jarrow, to the Tyne Tunnel. If Gateshead's bridge is 21st century, the Tyne Tunnel is very 1950s. It's austerity Britain, but it's also a confident and considerate Britain.

There's the two-lane vehicle tunnel, of course, but also its parallel companion: a double-barrelled shotgun propelling you under the river, one barrel for pedestrians only, the other for cyclists only. The cyclist's tunnel is 274.5m long, 3.7m in diameter, about 12m below the river bed, and about 50 years behind the times. The tunnel entrance, in Jarrow Riverside Park, is a perky little roundhouse that looks like it really ought to house an information centre, or perhaps feature in the dénouement of a low-budget 1960s science fiction film.

To descend the 25m to the tunnel you can take the lift, or use the 61m-long escalators. The tunnel itself is a time-capsule. Work began in 1939 but was interrupted by war; it was eventually opened in 1951, and that emerging postwar spirit is still there. It's a sparse affair, the tunnel, lined with gooseberry-and-cream coloured tiles apparently requisitioned from a municipal swimming pool, and starkly lit by a monorail of harsh, shadowless fluorescent strips.

It's all a bit grubby from the ages, touched up here and there with

when you see the magnificent Millennium Bridge greeting you. Now, to explore that renowned Newcastle nightlife...

■ Also in the area

A couple of kilometres east and southish from the south entrance of the tunnel is Bede's World, a museum dedicated to the life and work of the historian monk of 1300 years ago. About 4km downriver from the tunnel is the Shields Ferry, which will shuttle you and bike across the mouth of the Tyne for a pound. The harbour and pier areas are interesting to nose around by bike.

grout of various vintages, and decorated with rivulets of rusty stains. The sign says plainly *CYCLISTS TUNNEL* in an unfussy serif face – no apostrophe, but no mission statement or fancy logo either, thank goodness. It's a tunnel, an underwater siphon for ferry-dodging commuters, and it does exactly what it's supposed to, no more and no less. And it welcomes bikes.

In the closed-loop soundworld of the tunnel, the humming feedback of your tyres on the concrete flooring – especially if they're those knobbly mountain-bike ones – makes you feel as though you're being pursued by a rogue tram.

Out the other side, turn left and follow the signed cycle route (Hadrian's Wall) past the Roman fort upriver back to the train station. You're alongside roads mostly and don't see much of the river until you're back in the centre,

The cycle route alongside the north of the river is one branch of the wonderful Coast to Coast route (C2C, National Cycle Routes 7 and 71) from Workington/Whitehaven to Newcastle/Sunderland – see the Consett Maze entry on page 178.

Newcastle is a hub of several other long-distance cycle routes. The north entrance of the Tunnel is on the recently-completed Hadrian's Cycleway, National Cycle Route 72, that goes 280km from Tynemouth to Ravenglass. Pieces of Sustrans sculpture decorate the route from the tunnel. The Reivers Route runs west from Newcastle a similar distance along an alternative route to the west coast.

the tunnel itself is a time-capsule

The town is also on the Coasts and Castles route

(part of National Cycle Route 1, Newcastle to Edinburgh, 320km *(see Lindisfarne on page 190)* and the Three Rivers network (650km of car-free paths linking Middlesbrough, Hartlepool, Durham, Consett, Newcastle and South Shields).

Just as well Newcastle is so rich in bike paths: the Metro system runs all around here, but bikes are not allowed on it.

■ Other places like this

Putting aside tunnels on rail trails *(see Staple Hill, page 22)*, canals *(see Netherton, page 114)* and road underpasses, there are few cyclable tunnels in the UK, and very few dedicated cycling tunnels.

The 370m foot tunnel under the Thames at Greenwich has a similar look-and-feel to the Tyne Tunnel, and is part of Sustrans' National Cycle Route 1, but it's shared with pedestrians, and you have to push your bike. The Woolwich Foot

Tunnel, down river from Greenwich, is a similar structure, but longer *(see page 59)*.

The 750m-plus Clyde Tunnel in Glasgow has one-way cycle tunnels either side; they are square in cross-section, entered directly from ground level. The huge Queensway Tunnel under the Mersey is open to cyclists at a few non-peak hours *(see page 154)* but is full of fast noisy traffic.

There are several similarly modern and elegant (if non-tilting) new bridges on the cycling network. Examples include the one over the Nene 4km east of Peterborough; the Lune at Lancaster; the Usk in Newport town centre *(see page 127)*; and the Ouse at York *(see page 166)*. The one over the Thames in London, from Tate Modern to St Paul's is pedestrian-only but you can conveniently walk your bike over; at the north side, a glass 'inclinator' (angled lift) is there to take you and your bike down the steps to the waterfront path.

Snackstop
Baltic Mill Cafe. *Trendy cafe, with outside tables, in the Baltic building right beside the bridge.*

Bevvy break
Quayside Bar, by High Level Bridge. *Wetherspoon's pub, outside tables, views.*

Quirkshop
The Millennium Bridge tilts at various points most days (www.gateshead.gov.uk shows times). Opening and closing takes four or five minutes, and the bridge niftily cleans up its own litter: anything dropped on the deck rolls down into traps at the end during each elevation. On a Saturday night this may include some chips.

Tourer's tick list
✓ Newcastle's other bridges, nightlife
✓ Hadrian's Wall cycle route
✓ Bede's World

OS 88, grid ref NZ330658
INFO Gateshead Visitor Centre, St Mary's Church, Gateshead NE8 2AU, tel. 0191 478 4222, tourism@gateshead.gov.uk; www.tynetunnel.info

Consett Bike Maze

CONSETT MAZE

WHERE *Workington or Whitehaven to Newcastle or Sunderland (220km one way)*

WHAT *Challenging but achievable 3-4 day coast-to-coast odyssey on paths and roads*

WHY *Best long-weekend ride in Britain*

HOW *Train to Workington/Whitehaven, train back from Newcastle/Sunderland*

The Sustrans Sea to Sea route offers the best, most satisfying cycling long-weekend you can have (C2C, www.c2c-guide.co.uk). It stretches from Workington or Whitehaven (where many cyclists start by dipping their wheels in the harbour water) on the Cumbrian west coast to Sunderland or Newcastle on the east. Superbly planned and signed, it is deservedly the most popular mid-distance leisure cycling route in the country.

A unique cycle labyrinth on Britain's favourite bike route

The start and end points make a logical route, with a feeling of closure. The scenery is fabulous, ranging from lush Lake District landscapes to bleak Pennine tops to bustling city riversides. The time needed for the average casual cyclists – three or four days – makes it doable in a long weekend. It's a challenge, with a few long hills, but within reach of even the rustiest cyclist on the rustiest bike. Many do it for charity, and many do it year after year. You can get there by train conveniently. Several companies offer a transport facility, taking you and bikes to the start or from the finish, if you need to get back to the car or to a train station. Simply put, it's a must-do, and we've picked out just one of the countless highlights that you go through en-route that makes it so great: Consett's Bike Maze, a feature probably unique in Britain.

Unlike most mazes, Andy Goldsworthy's landscape artwork – entitled the Jolly Drover's Maze – is designed to help riders find their way through. And unless you count places such as the cycle-lane system around Vauxhall roundabout in London, this is the only bicycle maze in the country. Possibly the world. (Certainly you're not allowed to start cycling around Hampton Court maze, or any of the other 120 mazes open to the public in England that we know of.)

The Maze is in Leadgate, next to Consett in County Durham. If you're doing the C2C, you'll get there during your last day, heading for Sunderland rather than Newcastle; you're only a couple of cycling hours from the east coast. Just after a pub called the Jolly Drover's, on a busy roundabout, across the ring road the maze is through a hedge, and flagged by a metal signpost that looks like an upended electric hob that has been sprayed silver.

The main black gravel path suddenly starts to wiggle, as if plotted by a man wheeling a defective supermarket trolley, and dodges between head-high banks of earth. Off to the left, down any of the arcing valleys hemmed in by similar earthen walls, is the inside of the maze. Head off into any of the valleys to begin.

There is very little danger of getting lost in the labyrinth – in any case, clambering up a bank for a view from above is always an option for getting a fix on your position.

The object of Goldsworthy's design was to bring curious visitors into the heart of the maze, "leading the explorers on rather than losing them". Laid out in 1989 on the site of the old Eden Pit Colliery, the concentric layout of the earthen ridges is intended to mimic ripples spreading outwards on a pond.

The maze was a bit scruffy and weedy, as you can see from the pictures, when we last visited in autumn 2006. When it's tended and tidy, though, it can be lovely, as it was on our first visit early one previous summer.

If you want to experience the Consett Bike Maze without doing the entire C2C, there's no train station close by. Your best bet is to reach it by one of the traffic-free paths that connect with a station at somewhere like Newcastle, Durham or Chester-le-Street – see below.

the layout mimics ripples spreading outwards on a pond

Sunderland leg alone you cycle past another Goldsworthy earth piece, the Lambton Worm; Tony Cragg's Terris Novalis, a stunning set of giant scientific instruments commemorating the once-thriving steelworks that have long since closed; Sally Matthews's Beamish Shorthorns, a herd of cows wittily made from scrap metal parts; and many more.

Consett is something of a junction for cycle routes. From here, the C2C offers two alternatives: one goes to Newcastle, and the other (the section with the maze on it) to Sunderland. National Cycle Route 14 (Barnard Castle to South Shields) also goes through Consett; it's a rail trail so is welcomingly flat. The Three Rivers Route, using NCN 14, links Consett via an amazing network of over 600km of entirely traffic-free cycle paths with Middlesbrough, Stockton, Hartlepool, Durham, Newcastle and South Shields, including the Derwent walk, the Lanchester valley, and Wansbeck Estuary Art Trail.

Consett is also on a part of the National Cycle Byway, a system of signed routes on back lanes, tracks and byways (www.thenationalbyway.org). Part of it goes through Consett: a 180km self-contained circular route that takes you through Barnard Castle and Durham.

About 10km east of the maze along the C2C is Beamish, home to a large open-air museum that

■ Also in the area

There are countless other artworks on the C2C. On the Consett-

recreates working and everyday life in the 1800s and early 1900s. You can ride a 1920s tram, which is rather fun, but you'll be glad when you get your bike back.

■ Other places like this

There are several examples of turf mazes in England. They have no hedges or fences; they are simply patterns cut into the grass that form a small walkable maze. Obviously you can cheat by just stepping over to where you want to be. They're not cyclable, being too small in any case, but many make interesting elements of a day ride. The best is in Alkborough, Lincolnshire, just east of where the Rivers Trent and Ouse blunder in to each other. It's situated on an unexpected hill with a surprisingly commanding view of the confluence area, (now a flood-plain again) – perfect for a picnic. It's not far from the strange middle-of-nowhere Horkstow miniature sus-

pension bridge *(see page 161)*.

Another turf maze (or 'Julian's bower', as they might be referred to or marked on maps) is in Wing, Leicestershire. It's only a few kilometres from the agreeable one-day traffic-free circuit of Rutland Water *(see page 90)*. There is also a turf maze at Histon, outside Cambridge; and one next to the weir in the centre of Bath on the cyclable river towpath *(see page 18)*.

In general, Sustrans trails are packed with interesting trailside art, usually reflecting local character and heritage. They blend in with but also enhance the landscape, and often make you smile too (www.sustrans.org). Our favourites include planets at York *(see page 169)*, the DNA sequence at Cambridge *(see page 86)*, and the giant pencils just off the Bath-Bristol path at Mangotsfield *(see page 23)*.

Snackstop
The C2C takes you past a Sainsbury's in Consett, about three kilometres west of the maze. Stock up and picnic at the maze itself, or further on when you get some views. There are cafes in Consett, and in Beamish further up.

Bevvy break
Jolly Drovers, Leadgate, Consett. *On a humdrum roundabout, but right next to maze, and with outside tables.*

Quirkshop
Consett's steelworks are long gone, but a reminder of the old days is at Blackpool: it's said that from the top of the tower, you can 'see Consett': the name is stamped into every steel beam that makes up the structure, because they were all made in the town.

Tourer's tick list
✓ Beamish museum
✓ Artwork spotting
✓ Rail trails

OS 88, grid ref NZ133520
INFO www.sustrans.org.uk

www.BizarreBiking.com/Extras

Cam High Road

CAM HIGH ROAD

WHERE *North Yorkshire: Ribblehead to Bainbridge (18km one way)*

WHAT *Challenging offroad Dales ride with fabulous scenery*

WHY *Most exciting Roman road in Britain*

HOW *Train to Ribblehead*

This moderately tough day ride needs a tough bike – mountain bike or very sturdy tourer – but rewards you with a fabulously exciting ride through thrilling Dales landscape, and the country's most exciting Roman road.

An exciting Roman Road on the roof of the Yorkshire Dales

From Ribblehead station, head north-east up the B6255. After 3km turn right onto the stony track which soon climbs steeply; this is the worst surface of the route but it gets better. Near the top of the climb, at Cam End, the road straightens out. This is the Roman route, and from now it's mostly a straight line to Bainbridge, varying from fine thread of tarmac to farm track to bumpy bridleway.

Keep heading north-east. Where the tarmac road dives off downhill left, about 12km from Ribblehead, your route continues straight on as a track. Wether Fell is in front of you to your left, and in blue-sky weather, paragliders jump into the ether from near the summit.

Past the summit, as you go downhill, is some rocky stuff that roadologists believe is either the original Roman surface, or something from the road's refurbishment in frockcoat days as the Richmond-Lancaster turnpike. It must have been a rickety journey.

This last 5km is the most glorious bit. It has the kind of beeline straightness of those ironing-board landscapes south of the Severn-Trent line, but with the rugged verticality of the North. A Roman road fit for a Yorkshireman. You can imagine the late Fred Trueman's eighty-greats-grandfather holding forth about it all over an amphora or two: "T'Fosse Way? That in't a road, lad, it's a bloody promenade! You could walk that in ballet shoes! Now, Cam 'igh Road, that's a road, and wi' proper scenery an' all!"

So make no mistake: this is the Dales. It can be a rough old surface (fine for a full-suspension mountain bike, though), and in dodgy weather can be like facing Fred on a rain-affected pitch after he overheard you calling him a poof to your Oxbridge chums. But even in half-decent conditions this is a thrilling ride along arguably England's most exciting Roman Road, giving you big views of Wensleydale. It's very well preserved, and though the scenery may have changed quite a bit since then (we guess it was much more wooded in those pre-sheep-farm days) it has a feeling of unspoiled sweep and scope about it.

Indeed, it really does give you an impression of what it must have been like for the soldiers of 18 or 19 centuries ago, trudging back to their fort at Bainbridge after quelling another uprising of insurgent Brigantes. And after being bored to death in a tavern by some retired gladiator banging on about how

the Ure valley to Garsdale Head station – though that would involve at least 8km of the A684 main road.

Also in the area

From Bainbridge is a scenic, but slightly hilly circuit of England's shortest river, the Bain. It flows only 3km or so from the natural lake of Semer Water down into Bainbridge and the River Ure. It's roughly parallel to Cam High Road and is apparently a very good fishing spot for wild brown trout. For the river circuit from Bainbridge, take the lane that becomes the Cam High Road, but follow the tarmac left. That will lead you to the village of Countersett and Semer Water, the largest natural lake in Yorkshire, but still only about 5km-6km all the way around, making it a good cycling detour. Crossing over the Bain, take a left back towards Bainbridge. You can now tick off England's shortest riverside cycle route, both ways,

much better everything was at the exact time he happened to be in his early twenties, and how they were all characters then and now it's all about money.

A final tarmac descent takes you into Bainbridge. In the vast village green finding space for a picnic, or perhaps a spontaneous game of polo, is unlikely to present a problem. There are also some old stocks, where you can

an impression of what it was like for soldiers of 18 centuries ago

indulge in photographic amusement. In ancient times it's said that a Bainbridge horn blower sounded his horn to summon foresters and travellers back to the safety of the village. The horn (which hangs in the Rose & Crown) is still sounded at 10pm every night from the 27th of September to Shrove Tuesday.

To get back to a train station, you have to either retrace your steps to Ribblehead, or cycle west 15km up

as well as having ridden all the way round Yorkshire's closest approximation of Lake Superior.

Wensleydale cheese, famed from the Wallace and Gromit animations, is made in Hawes, 6km west of Bainbridge (go along the minor road to the north of the Ure rather than the A684 to the south). There's a visitor centre at Wensleydale Dairy in the town.

Hardy cyclists might consider

cycling the tough, steep, thrilling road north from Hawes to Thwaite over Buttertubs Pass, and on north through Keld. About 20km from Hawes is the remote, remarkable Tan Hill Inn, at 528m high claimed to be England's highest pub. You can get married here.

For other cycling opportunities in the Dales, see the Dentdale entry on page 170.

■ Other places like this

There are any number of Roman roads that are now bridleways or other traffic-free routes, as a glance at OS maps will show.

Some of the most scenic are in Wales, near Brecon. This was a Roman fiveways, the junction of many routes. If you're mountain biking the wonderful Beacons, or doing Sustrans' Lôn Las Cymru route, pause to explore the Roman roads round here – look for the straight lines on OS 160 and head along Mynydd Illtud. They centre on Y Gaer, an old Roman camp just west of Brecon, and the remains of Y Pigwn, halfway between here and Llandovery, are interesting to nose round. Here too is a Sarn Helen, an old-road name that is found elsewhere in Wales.

The 3D tarmac route from Langdale to Eskdale over Wrynose and Hardknott Passes in the Lake District – once cited as England's most severe road by Guinness – is, surprisingly, a Roman road. Churned up by the tanks which used it to practise three-point turns while shooting at things, it was only surfaced after World War II. Hardknott is thrilling cycling – if it's not raining too hard, which it always has been when we've been there – but the road is shared with car drivers and motorcyclists *(see page 153)*.

The Fosse Way ride *(see page 106)* lists a number of other notable Roman roads.

Snackstop

The Chippy, Main St, Hawes. *If you're used to soggy, tasteless pub fish and chips, this will be a very pleasant surprise: delicious fresh fish, crispy light batter, perky and substantial chips. Eat it on the bench outside the shop with fellow diners, probably happily retired, in walking gear and ready for a chat, in this typical Dales town.*

Bevvy break

Rose & Crown, Bainbridge. *Big, friendly 15th-century coaching inn on the village green. Outside tables.*

Quirkshop

Wensleydale Creamery, just south of Hawes's market place, is the only place in the world that makes real Wensleydale cheese. Visitor centre and Cheese Experience tour.

Tourer's tick list

✓ Ribblehead Viaduct
✓ Settle-Carlisle railway
✓ Dales town feel
✓ See sheepdogs in action

OS 98, grid ref SD 925895
INFO Hawes Tourist Information, Dales Centre, Hawes, North Yorks DL8 3NT, tel. 01969 667450

Great Dun Fell

GREAT DUN FELL

WHERE *North Yorkshire: Appleby to Great Dun Fell summit (30km return)*

WHAT *Smooth tarmac road, mostly traffic free, with big climb*

WHY *Britain's highest road, cyclable but banned to traffic*

HOW *Train to Appleby*

This tough but rewarding climb in Pennine hill scenery takes you as high as you can go on a road in Britain: on a little-known road that is open to cyclists, but banned to traffic, and which takes you to 858m, the summit of Great Dun Fell.

Britain's highest road 848m up and no cars allowed

Start from Appleby, a pleasant market town on the mildly awesome Carlisle-Settle railway. Follow signs to Dufton, north out of the town, through the village (where there's a youth hostel) and on to Knock. Take the first right after that – it's signposted 'Knock Christian Centre', which is appropriate because in a few minutes, some praying might be in order. From here to the top of the Fell is about 7km, and 630m of relentless climb.

The lane is straight and rises gently, then abruptly, just before a sign warning of no public access beyond that point. It's a service road, built for vehicles having business at the radar establishment on the summit of the hill – but it also happens to be a bridleway, so you're perfectly entitled to carry on cycling. The road continues, very steeply, to the left, then calms down and straightens out with expansive views to the left. Then it turns right, climbs sharply and winds again, past a lot of panicky sheep. Again it straightens, beaming to the head of the valley, where the stream rises up to meet you.

There is a sign for the radar establishment – though in misty weather you may bump into it first – and a track joins on the left. Carry straight on, up and farther up. After a bend left, the bridleway (the Pennine Way) carries on to the right, and the road forks left, blocked by a barrier. This road continues to the summit, where the spooky giant golfball of the radar

installation is studded with saucepan-shaped satellite receivers.

Here you're 858m high, on the second-highest summit in the Pennines (Cross Fell is the highest at 893m) – and yet you can cycle here on a shopping bike. Compare that to the Khyber Pass between Pakistan and Afghanistan, which only reaches 1080m. You're also much higher than the highest stretch of motorable road in all of Britain (the A93 at Glenshee in Scotland, 670m) and almost high enough to see Denmark (highest road, 172m).

There may well be fine views out to the southern Lakes on a good day, and it may well be a wonderful place for the picnic nestling snug in your panniers. Both times I've been though, the Pennines have been wrapped in ghostly stratus; I groped around the top sprayed by that curious sort of sharp, fine rain that falls in all directions, including upwards, and saw nothing except the immediate few metres of tarmac. So check

the weather forecast before you go. And then go anyway.

There's no way from here except down, though on a good day this should be a hoot, as there's unlikely to be anything coming up. And the surface, unmolested by cars, is in pretty good nick. You might even be able to freewheel it all, if you have enough momentum and breeze behind you at the sections where it goes up a bit. You might reckon on 75 minutes or so from Knock village to the summit, about 10 minutes for the descent back, and about 30 to get your breath back in between.

From Knock, retrace your steps to Appleby.

reckon on 75 minutes to the summit, 10 minutes for the descent back

Boroughgate, is worth spending a bit of time in. The town has a castle (which is currently closed), a jazz festival in July, and a famous Gypsy horse fair in June, which is attended by thousands of travellers.

Sustrans Pennine Cycleway, running 580km from Derby to Berwick (National Cycle Route 68) goes through Appleby and past Knock. South from Appleby it goes to Settle with spurs to Kirky Stephen and Kendal; north it goes up to Haltwhistle, Bellingham, Wooler and Berwick, www.cycle-routes.org /penninecycleway.

The Lakes are only an hour or two's ride west, so you could always tag Dun Fell on to a few days' jaunt round there. One stop up the rail line from Appleby (the Settle-Carlise railway) is Langwathby, which is crossed by the C2C route *(see Consett Bike Maze entry on page 178)*. The

■ Also in the area

Appleby, with its fine old buildings in the market street of

Pennine Cycleway north also crosses the C2C, if you want to join it by cycling there.

If you like challenging offroad stuff, there are lots of mountain biking opportunities round here. You're not too far here from Britain's most enjoyable long downhill *(see page 170)* and most exciting Roman Road *(see page 118)*; access both of those by stations on the Carlisle-Settle line.

■ Other places like this

The highest you can get on a surfaced public road in England appears to be 627m, which occurs at two places, neither of them far from here. One is on the A689 near Nenthead in the Pennines, at Killhope Cross. Nenthead is on the C2C route from Whitehaven / Workington to Sunderland / Newcastle *(see page 178)*, so you can dodge off for a couple of minutes to collect Killhope. Instead of turning left off the main road a couple of minutes out of town, stay straight on; Killhope summit is a few metres beyond. The other tarmac top of that height is on an unclassified road about 14km due east of Dun Fell, vaulting the hills between the villages of St John's Chapel and Langdon Beck. (A parallel, unsurfaced road to its north-east out of Ireshopeburn goes up to 674m, evidently the highest through-route in England.)

For the really ambitious with very knobbly tyres, here's a bridleway to the summit of Snowdon (1085m). This is clearly the highest point you can get on a bike in England and Wales, because it is the highest point in England and Wales. However, there are voluntary bans on using it at weekends, and in any case most mountain bikers say other routes in Snowdonia are more satisfying. The rack-and-pinion train to the top doesn't take bikes, unfortunately, so no train-up-cycle-down trickery here.

Snackstop
Lady Anne's Pantry, Bridge St, Appleby. *Friendly local place in a town where you're spoilt for choice.*

Bevvy break
Royal Oak, Bongate, Appleby. *17th-century coaching inn close to River Eden. Real ales and large gravel forecourt to sit outside by your bike.*

Quirkshop
The organ in St Lawrence church in Appleby is said to be the oldest still played in the country: it dates from 1683, so wasn't built with all this modern music, like Bach, in mind.

Tourer's tick list
✓ Picnic at top of Dun Fell
✓ Appleby town centre
✓ Carlisle-Settle railway

OS 91, grid ref NY710322
INFO Appleby Tourist Information, Moot Hall, Boroughgate, Appleby-in-Westmorland, Cumbria CA16 6XE, tel. 017683 51177, tic@applebytown.org.uk

VISIT HISTORIC

LINDISFARNE ABBEY.

Lindisfarne

Where the famous Bible was!

LINDISFARNE

WHERE *Northumberland: Berwick to Lindisfarne (30km one way)*

WHAT *Quiet country lanes*

WHY *Ride famous causeway to Holy Island that's submerged twice a day*

HOW *Train to Berwick*

This ride along gentle country lanes south out of Berwick takes you onto one of Britain's most remarkable roads: the causeway to Holy Island, or Lindisfarne. Start from Berwick and follow the National Cycle Route 1 signs south. They take you along traffic-free coastal paths for a few kilometres before cutting inland to a rather circuitous route along minor roads. You go through the village of Beal and on a brief car-free track to the beginning of the causeway.

Bikes are the best way to enjoy the celebrated causeway

There, across the water, is Holy Island, connected to the mainland by a kilometre and a half of tarmac road. Twice a day, the sea gradually rolls in over the marshy surrounding sands and envelops the causeway. Lindisfarne becomes Wholly Island.

There's a small car park and some information boards listing Safe Crossing Times for the next few days. A few hundred metres along the causeway is a wooden box on stilts. This is the refuge for overcasual timekeepers who have unexpectedly gone paddling. It's a cosy little place, but five hours in it might get tedious. It has a door, bench, south-facing window, emergency phone, and lists of taxi and car hire firms in case your intended means of transport is now inconveniently floating towards another Shipping Forecast area.

Do your homework, and choose a day when the last Safe Crossing Time for an incoming tide is in the afternoon. Schedule your arrival to allow an hour or two on the island before the last SCT. From the mainland to the island's village centre it's only about 20 minutes' ride. But aim to start cycling back around the last Safe Crossing Time. They err very much on the side of caution; you'll have well over an hour to do your 20-minute return trip before any part of the road gets remotely moist.

Safely back on the mainland, curious onlookers will be gathering to watch the tide come in, especially if it's a sunny weekend. The stretch between here and the refuge is the

lowest-lying, and the one that goes under first. You can dawdle your way up and back several times to the refuge, crossing the small bridge that crosses a creek just before it, and watch the water infiltrate the sands imperceptibly. It's hard to believe that the whitehorse breakers you can see on the distant north horizon will ever make it this far. But two hours from now they certainly will.

There'll be a regular procession of cars blithely ignoring the Safe Crossing Times. You can see why they're tempted. Over an hour after the SCT, the water might only just be lapping on to the blacktop, and its progress might seem as gentle as a paddling pool filled from a watering-can. Some of the late crossers are clearly locals who know the tides like the back of their hand, and exactly how hairy both can be. Others are daytrippers pushing their luck, some to ludicrously risky

The big-skied roll across the causeway to Lindisfarne is a special experience in itself: the grassy dunes and sands are a nature reserve, and there's that salty-breezed, North-Sea feel to the landscape similar to that of the Danish and Dutch coasts. On the island itself, you have a range of possibilities: visit the Castle, go nature-trailing, watch birds, toy with the idea of intentionally stranding yourself in the pub, whatever.

lengths. You can feel smug about how corrosive that salt water is for their car as they slosh through it in a panicked dash for safety. Remember to rinse off your chainset though, or two days later, it'll turn russet and attract corncrakes with its grating.

Aquaplane happily around, and see which car drivers get caught. Stick to the area between the refuge and the mainland, where observers hopeful to see the refuge become occupied will be. The waves nibble away at the road, gradually turning asphalt into marine biology.

Quite a sight. If the tide only came in once a year, it would be a must-see natural phenomenon on a par with a solar eclipse. The fact that it happens so regularly and so predictably shouldn't make it any less awesome.

Retracing your steps to Berwick makes for a long day; stay on the island if you can.

aquaplane happily around, and see which car drivers get caught

Berwick is a visitable town, a curious Scottish-English hybrid with characterful buildings of grey, pink and brown stone, and a splendid collection of historic civil engineering on the Tweed. The majestic 28-arch railway viaduct, built in 1850 by Robert Stephenson, carries the main line to Scotland; you cycle under it as you come into the town. Cross the Tweed northwards by the expansive concrete bridge of 1928, which has broad bike lanes both sides; then, more atmospherically, cross it southwards on the adjacent single-lane (and one-way) pink arched bridge of 1634. Take a circuit of the town's impressive city walls; you may have to push your bike on some bits.

South of Holy Island is the rugged Northumbrian coast, known for mighty castles: Alnwick,

Bamburgh, Belsay Hall, Dunstanburgh, Norham, Prudhoe, Warkworth. This is good biking country, and Sustrans' Coasts and Castles route takes you past the highlights, including Holy Island, in its 300km odyssey between the Forth and Tyne. National Cycle Route 1 goes on south to Dover, or north to John O'Groats.

■ Other places like this

Another, little-known, low-tide-only community in England is the small Lancashire village of Sunderland. (Don't get stranded there if you need a pub: the nearest is at Overton, on the other side of the water.) At nearby Morecambe Bay is a 12km- long low-tide road marked across the vast, flat sands. But disorienting mists and lethal lightning tides make it strictly for experienced locals only: you need a guide. Even OS maps carry stark warnings.

Britain's other famous semi-off-shore spiritual site is St Michael's Mount, way down in south-east Cornwall. It is possible to cycle the natural causeway from Marazion, although it's very bumpy. The castle is a National Trust property.

The marshy margins of Essex have several tidal crossings over the gravy-and-mash coastline: the low-water hop across the Crouch between Hullbridge and South Woodham Ferrers, for example. There are also wet roads to Osea, Mersea and Horsey Islands (the last being the one featured in *Swallows and Amazons*). None of the three are marked on the OS map as a right of way, though. There's a short part-time footpath over the sand to the hotel on Burgh Island, near Kingsbridge, in south Devon. When tides permit, it might be cyclable to the island where the elegantly archaic art-deco hotel serves cocktails, and there's the cosy 14th century Pilchard Inn.

Snackstop
Pilgrims Cafe, Holy Island. *Real coffee in Lindisfarne village centre.*

Quirkshop
Ship Inn, Holy Island. *Enjoy a Holy Island Bitter or other cask ale right by the castle and 'harbour'.*

Quirkshop
Most sacred books were produced by teams, but in the early 700s, one Lindisfarne monk, Eadfrith, executed all the Celtic, Christian and eastern influenced calligraphy and embellishments in one of England's great artistic and religious treasures, the Lindisfarne Gospels. It's no longer on Holy Island – see it at the British Library in London.

Tourer's tick list
✓ Lindisfarne castle and priory
✓ Lindisfarne mead from St Aiden's winery
✓ Berwick bridges
✓ Coastal castles

OS 75, grid ref NU080427
INFO Berwick Tourist Information, 26 Marygate, Berwick TD15 1DT, tel. 01289 330733, tourism@berwick-upon-tweed.gov.uk. Safe crossing times at www.northumberlandlife.org/holy-island/default.asp or from 01289 389200

CRITICAL MASS

WHERE *London: From the National Theatre to somewhere else (roughly 10km)*

WHAT *Unplanned mass ride round London streets*

WHY *Curious social event, half-ride, half-demo*

HOW *Train to Waterloo*

This is an odd one: an unplanned ride with no destination, no organisation, and no fixed route. The only thing you can be certain about Critical Mass is that the last Friday of every month, under Waterloo bridge on London's South Bank by the National Theatre, several hundred cyclists will gather. At around 7pm they'll move off slowly en masse, on their way... somewhere.

It's nice to be in charge of the roads for a change

Critical Mass is one of those things that you simply have to do, if only the once, if for no other reason than to have your own firm views on it one way or the other. It divides opinion: ask ten London cyclists what they think of CM and you'll get ten different answers. (In contrast, ask ten taxi drivers and they'll all give you much the same answer, unlikely to be positive.)

To the participating cyclist, it's a spontaneous, peaceful, non-political gathering every month, when – for a change – we control a few streets, for a few minutes. The boot is on the other foot, and it's pedalling instead of jabbing an accelerator. Hundreds of bicycles, sometimes over a thousand, reclaim the streets from the cars, trucks and buses. Wherever the peloton passes, traffic has to wait until it has cleared. So there. Riding London's usually chaotic and dangerous roadmap becomes a pleasure instead: that whole bridge to ourselves; that stretch of dual carriageway free of traffic, with nothing but bikes. In numbers associated with Beijing streets of old, cyclists can dominate the junctions in communal safety, briefly free of the predatory internal combustion engine.

A CM ride is an exercise in Brownian-motion randomness. It might go twice round Waterloo roundabout, cross the bridge, hold up the Strand briefly, circuit Parliament Square, pass by Buckingham Palace, thread under Wellington Arch... Or something completely different.

The pro-CM view is that riding by chance en masse through London's streets shows there are a lot of us, a force to be taken seriously. CM doubters point out that some participants confound this: they provoke motorists by pointedly holding them up and shouting. Most motorists react with stoicism, though a few impatient bullies try to push through – only to find themselves instantly surrounded by dozens or even hundreds of cyclists. For once, the tyrant in the car can't get their own way by force. However much they sound their horn or swear, they simply have to wait.

It's hard to feel much sympathy with motorists who complain that CM 'blocks up the traffic'. Traffic already does that, far more effectively all by itself. In fact, it seems from the saddle as if car drivers have their own CM every day of the year, gathering in a non-organised way to blockade roads and wreak sclerotic mayhem.

ence manage to keep order without being pro- or anti- anyone. It's worth coming along, just to watch the parade of bikes.

■ Also in the area

This is the nearest you get to playing bike-Monopoly: through a conspiracy of Chance and Community Chest you advance to Mayfair, go to Trafalgar Square, take a trip to Marylebone Station, or go back to Old Kent Road (rare). Finding your way home through the backstreets after a CM can be one of the most enjoyable parts of the evening.

With no fixed endpoint to the 'ride' (sometimes Trafalgar Square; and it lasts till roughly 8pm or 9pm) you can peel off any time you've had enough. As the route is unplanned you might find yourself anywhere in central London, so have a street map handy.

The area where riders convene for London Critical Mass, just under Waterloo Bridge, is worth visiting any day in summer. Artificial grass goes down on the tennis-court-sized flat area in front of the National Theatre, and there's free outdoor entertainment every afternoon and evening. It's weird and wonderful stuff – avant-garde street theatre from Catalonia, Brazilian samba bands, Freddie Mercury tribute comedians, Russian clowns, and things you couldn't

But going on a Mass can be sociable and fun (so long as you're not behind a cyclist with a sound system playing infernally loud music), and has to be done at least once. An entertaining range of tattoos and facial iron is on show in summer. People display piercings in some intimate and normally inaccessible places – just under Lambeth Bridge, for example. Participants range from dreadlocked types with an interest in organically grown herbs to power-suited city slickers. Many forms of human-powered transport join in, from skateboards to wheelchairs to inline skates.

And the full gamut of bike types take part:

the nearest you get to playing bike-Monopoly

folders, top-end tourers, ancient basket-and-bell shoppers, couriers' 'fixies', flash high-budget road bikes, tricycles, unicycles, tandems, recumbents, cycle rickshaws – and police cyclists, who in our experi-

make up. Absolutely ideal for viewing over a picnic or a bottle of chilled white, and there are sturdy bike racks just around the corner.

From under Waterloo Bridge you can cycle up and down the South Bank along the river any distance in either direction, though it's often crowded with tourists.

■ Other places like this

Critical Mass rides take place in many large towns round the world. They originated in San Francisco in 1992 and have been going in London since 1994. In our experience, London's event is most similar in atmosphere to the original San Franciscan gatherings. The website www.critical-mass.org has a list of dates and places around the world with CMs: there are over 150 listed in Europe and over 200 in north America.

There are a few sporadic attempts at Masses outside London, with varying degrees of success. If you're in a small town don't be surprised if just you, a middle-aged hippie, a chirpy young Aussie woman, and a rather embarrassed chap in a suit cycle up to reclaim the streets. We once took part in a Critical Mass in Auckland, New Zealand, which was even less well-attended than that. Perhaps Auckland just has better things to do in the early evening.

So, there may or may not be a Mass coming up this month or next, in Bath, Birmingham, Bradford, Brighton, Bristol, Cambridge, Cardiff, Chester, Colchester, Coventry, Exeter, Guildford, Hastings, Kidderminster, Lancaster, Leeds, Liverpool, Manchester, Newbury, Newcastle, Norwich, Oxford, Preston, Reading, Sheffield, Stoke, Walsall, Wolverhampton, Worcester or York; an Internet search is your best bet for finding out more details.

Snackstop

Cafe, South Bank. *You may not have the time or inclination for a coffee and cake on a Friday evening, but if so there's the National Theatre cafe right there.*

Bevvy break

BFI Bar, South Bank. *International brands of premium lager rather than microbrewery cask ale, but handy.*

Quirkshop

What it is about juggling I don't know, but events like this always seem to have a signifcantly larger component of people exercising circus skills than average. If you want a free lesson in the rudiments of three-ball juggling from one of your friendly fellow CMers, this is not a bad place to come. Just keep thinking 'throw-throw, catch-catch'.

Tourer's tick list

✓ Just go with the flow

OS 176, grid ref T Q307803
INFO No official information source exists as CM is not 'organised', but www.criticalmasslondon.org.uk is one of several websites about the ride

CRAP CYCLE LANES

WHERE   *London: Battersea to Vauxhall (2km)*

WHAT   *Bike path on Nine Elms Lane*

WHY   *Britain's worst cycle lane?*

HOW   *Train to Battersea Park or Queenstown Road*

his is the shortest route in the book, but the funniest: an example of the appalling nonsense that some councils believe are 'cycle facilities'. It takes you from near Battersea Park, just south of the river in west London, to Vauxhall; but rather than the destinations, it's the grim comedy value of the route that we're interested in.

Meet Britain's worst cycle lane – or do you know worse?

Start from Battersea Park or Queenstown Road stations, and head east along Battersea Park Road, past the Dogs and Cats Home and the Power Station on your left. The cycle lane starts on the bridge over the railway, as a marked-off portion of the footpath. However, you can't actually cycle on to it, because it's blocked off with barricades; you would have to stop on the road and lift your machine over the festive red-and-white metre-high plastic blocks.

Then, like any good comic monologue, the 'cycle path' embarks on a long amusing meander along the footpath. The white line marking out the 'cycle path's' territory seems painted by one of those drunks taking a random walk in a first-year undergraduate mathematical problem, as it slaloms its way around bus shelters, trees, lampposts, and sometimes theoretical obstacles visible only to the befuddled council employees who were entrusted with the paintbrush.

At times it disappears altogether, re-emerging further on transporter-beam fashion, like a doomed minor character in a Star Trek expedition. The climax comes as you approach Vauxhall, just as the new Covent Garden fruit warehouses come into view on your right. The 'cycle path' is entirely blocked by an electrics box and support pole for a CCTV camera. Just beyond it, your progress along the 'cycle path' is halted completely by the sign for the 'cycle path', thanks to its being placed right in the middle of the 'cycle path'. Finally you're at Vauxhall roundabout, where you can take a train out of here. Except that the cycle path round the roundabout is discontinuous and cumbersome, forcing you to stop every three metres... If you ever did a paper round as a teenager, this stop-start regime may induce a tear of nostalgia. There's a fast cycle subway under the railway line, with a witty little right-angle blind bend at the end − presumably to help introduce local cyclists to each other, through sudden impact and subsequent exchange of addresses and insurance schemes.

Unfortunately, there are all too many cycle paths like Nine Elms Lane. Ones that provide parking for Royal Mail vans, sidings for unattended roadwork equipment, and freehold for a phone box and a his-

toric tree. Glittering examples of council planning – but only glittering because of all the broken glass catching the sunlight, which they have no will or legal obligation to clear away. And some motorists wonder why cyclists use the road instead...

So get out there and start collecting examples near you with your mobile phone camera or digital snapper. Gather the evidence. Amuse your friends, embarrass the council, give the local paper a story. Who knows, you might just persuade the council to invest properly, get some advice from local cycling groups, and produce facilities that actually encourage people on two wheels. That would be to everybody's benefit.

start collecting examples near you, and email them to CrapCycleLanes@ eye-books.com

Putney, picking up the Thames path west *(see page 58).*

Heading east from Vauxhall, you can cycle almost all along the riverside as far as Greenwich and even Dartford *(see Woolwich Ferry entry on page 62).*

In London, you can join London Cycle Campaign (lcc.org.uk) to help make things better. There are also lively Borough groups, which arrange lots of rides ranging from the investigation of facilities to the purely social. As much campaigning goes on at a local level, these may be a good start if you want to make a difference locally. LCC's website has a list of Borough groups and contacts.

For finding your way around London's cycle facilities, the free maps produced by Transport for London are very useful. Pick up some or all of the 14 London Cycling Guides in the series from any London bike shop; or request a copy from the cycling section from the TfL website (www.tfl.gov.uk); or call 020 7222 1234. The maps are based on the maps you see in A to Z guides, but without a street index, and with cycle paths and routes marked on it. The Nine Elms Lane facilities are marked in brown, which seems appropriate.

■ Also in the area

To see what cycle routes should be like, hop on the westward train at Queenstown Road or Vauxhall and get off five minutes up the line at

■ Other places like this

Warrington Cycle Campaign's website runs a regular 'Facility of the

Month' section, highlighting particularly stupid examples of cycle paths (for details visit them at www.warringtoncyclecampaign.co.uk). You can see a collection of the worst in the book, *50 Crap Cycle Lanes*, published by Eye Books. All the bad-lane cliches are here: lanes blocked by the sign for the lane, lanes that are blocked by fences and letter boxes, lanes too narrow for a pipe-cleaner man on a diet, lanes shorter than the length of a bike, and more.

But you won't have to go far to find equally absurd examples of your own. Terrible bike lanes – like burnt-out cars, beds of nettles, or mysteriously discarded small items of clothing – can be found as part of all too many cycle routes throughout the country. You'll find something near you just as entertaining as the Nine Elms example detailed above.

If you feel inspired to campaign for better cycling facilities on a national level, join the CTC, the national cyclists' organisation (Cycle Touring and Campaigning, www.ctc.org.uk). Members enjoy free third party insurance, a bi-monthly magazine, invitations to over a thousand cycling events each year, route and touring information, technical and product advice, cycle-related legal advice, discounts on bike purchases, and access to special holidays and tours.

Snackstop
Madeira Cafe. *Portuguese cafe 200m beyond Vauxhall, under the railway arches. Uniformly fabulous paninis, croissants, sandwiches, cakes, tarts – the fish is fantastic – and great coffee.*

Bevvy break
Masons Arms, Battersea Park Road. *By Battersea Park station, a typical London urbanites' pub with premium beers, good quality if pricey food, and a couple of outside tables.*

Quirkshop
Battersea Park is just behind you, with cycle paths and traffic-free lanes round its lake and along the riverfront – and its Peace Pagoda, a little bit of Asia in south London.

Tourer's tick list
✓ Comedy snap for local paper
✓ Letter to councillor
✓ Join local cycling campaign
✓ Get puncture repair kit

OS 1–204 inclusive, passim
INFO www.warringtoncyclecampaign.co.uk

WEIRD BIKES

WHERE *Your local bike shop*

WHAT *Folding bikes; recumbents; tandems etc*

WHY *Fun to try, but may just add a new element to your cycling*

HOW *Hire one for a day*

The standard diamond-frame bike has proved an astonishingly durable design. A chain-store mountain bike that sells for £99 is recognisably the same thing as Starley's Rover Safety Bicycle of 1885. Thanks to advances in engineering and production methods though, it will probably only last a tenth as long.

Folders, recumbents, tandems: try it, you might like it

However, there are many types of bicycle. Some are better than others for particular applications, like mixed-mode commuting, long-distance touring, or making people laugh. If you've never tried riding a recumbent, taking a folder on a city break, or wobbling along with your partner on a tandem, you should. Here's why...

Tandems

'Tandem' is one of those intrinsically funny words doomed to spend its life inhabiting the punchline of mechanically rendered jokes, like 'wombat' or 'trouser press'.

Nevertheless, riding a tandem is quite funny the first time, particularly for the Saturday shoppers watching. Wobbling around the bike shop car park as if the frame were made out of some experimental aluminium/custard alloy, for the stoker (the one at the back) the sensation of immobile handlebars is very odd. Once you get the feel of going in a straight line, however, you'll notice that there's only the wind resistance of one bike but with two people pedalling. The captain though (the one at the front) always has the lingering suspicion that they are actually doing all the work.

For most riders, tandems are huge fun to try, but of no practical use, like trouser presses; they're also impossible to take on trains. They do come into their own in some circumstances, though. For a couple engaged in long-distance touring, for example. Tandems can be an efficient way to get two people and their luggage to Turkmenistan or Tring, particularly if one contributes rather less legwork than the other. They also help riders with impaired vision or other cycling-unfriendly conditions to get about on two wheels.

To try out a tandem, hire one for a day trip on one of those flat, traffic-free railtrails such as the Camel Trail, the Tissington, or the Thames Path *(see page 58)*. The cost of renting one for the day may be the same as for two standard bikes, so it's well worth a go. The Camel Trail, Padstow Cycle Hire is right on the South Quay at the start of the trail and does a day's tandem for £20 (www.padstowcyclehire.com, 01841 533533); Parsley Hay is similarly well sited for the Tissington (www.peakdistrict.gov.uk/ index/visiting/cycle.htm, £30, 01298 84493). They may offer child-bike add-ons if you fancy a family road train.

The best option for Thames Path tandeming is London Recumbents in Battersea Park (£12 per hour, londonrecumbents.com, 0207 498 6453). There are a few kilometres of city streets and roads before the traffic-free paved stretch to Windsor, but you can get the feel of the machine in the park's network of car-free tarmac paths first.

A list of places hiring tandems is at www.tandem-club.org.uk, the website of the UK Tandem Club.

Recumbents

Recumbents come in all sorts of shapes, even tandem versions, but the essential difference from standard bikes is the riding position, lying back: the pedals, out in front perhaps at eye level, take none of your bodyweight. Some recumbents look much like normal bikes, only flatter, and with an armchair instead of a saddle; others might have three wheels, some are odd-sized, or have counter-intuitive stuff like under-bum handlebars.

There are two reasons to have a recumbent. One is efficiency and comfort: though their design sounds involved, they transmit leg power to the wheels, more travel for less effort; plus the position avoids saddle soreness and back twinges. Many serious ultra-long-distance tourers use recumbents. The low-slung profile, almost invisible to the wind, cuts down effort further. However, they're almost invisible to traffic as well, and wobblier away from the lights, so few people relish busy urban cycling on them.

But the main reason to have a recumbent is to decorate it. For some reason, perhaps the laid-back physical attitude translates into a mental one, recumbents end up lavishly accessorised: trip computers, radios, furry linings, picnic baskets, wi-fi laptops, minibars, jacuzzis etc.

Your best bet to try a recumbent is to hire one in a park for a day, where you can oscillate in safety. In London that might mean London Recumbents again, in Dulwich or

Battersea Park – see above. A Google search may locate somewhere nearer you.

Unicycles

Learning to ride a unicycle is one of those things best done in the privacy of a back garden, and starter models go from £99; call 0800 980 0711, or see www.unicycle.uk.com. Unbelievably, offroad unicycles are also built for downhilling.

Folding bikes

Folders are the most familiar non-standard bike. They seem to defy some unwritten natural law of transportation resources: horses aren't collapsible after all. Yet the same machine that can transport you round the world – or at least to the Circle Line – shrinks in seconds to a satchel full of modern sculpture. Thanks to more of us having to travel more often, gridlocked city centres, and limited bike spaces on trains, folders have enjoyed something of a boom in the last ten years. There are over 50 models currently available, and the celebrated Brompton is the model seen most in central London, often pedalled by well-to-do city types.

Some advantages of a folder are obvious (take the train, bus, taxi etc at liberty, save money and time by not driving). Some are less so (it's stealproof – you take it with you into the restaurant; fits in cramped attic flat; high resale value; saddle/handlebar adjustability and low crossbar that means a whole family can use the same

bike). Some advantages, only your closest friends might know (you can pedal wearing a long skirt).

The only disadvantage is the cost – £500–£600 for a decent one.

For a commute with a lot of stairs, portability is as important as foldability. Neatness of folding, with no sticky-out bits, is a must on crowded buses or trains.

Folder touring is also quite possible, and fun. I know, having cycled (-ish) halfway across Japan on a Brompton. They fold up so small they can fit into a Japanese phone box, should you require – and, incredible but true, they can even just about fit inside a typical Japanese apartment.

You have to travel light with a folder – not much more than a day-pack, travelling range is limited – perhaps half what you'd do on a standard bike, and steep hills or offroading aren't practical. Spares are a problem, too, but consider the advantages. If you're tired, it's raining, you get a puncture, or it gets dark or hilly or just boring – no problem. Dismantle the donkey and catch a bus, hop on a train or hitch a lift. You can cheat magnificently, taking cable cars up mountains and freewheeling down. Your bike can sleep in your hotel room. You can enjoy what would otherwise be bike-unfriendly cheap city breaks, by coach or budget flight. And it brings a talking point with locals, who are always curious to see the handbag-horse magic.

Trying out a folder is easy: most bike shops have one or two available for test-drive. Don't buy one simply because it folds nicely or

quickly, though; rent one for a day, and test-ride it in traffic. It'll only cost about £15. This is a small price to pay for developing the 3D spatialisation skills needed to grapple with a Brompton that seems unwilling to unfold. (The trick is to lift up the saddle first.)

Some shops hire a folding bike, and if you decide to keep it, the rental cost is knocked off the purchase price. Action Bikes in London SW1 (www.actionbikes.co.uk, 020 7799 2233), for instance, does it for £50 a week. It's an excellent way to see if a folder fits into your lifestyle, as well as the cupboard under the stairs.

Multi-person bikes

Funnier yet than tandems, as per the 'trandem' chaotically navigated by 1970s TV comedy trio the Goodies. For extreme amusement value, you might be able to hire a 'conference bike', with seven or more people facing in a circle inwards. Unwieldy to store and transport, they're hard to get hold of. Finding one inevitably involves a paper-chase of websites and phone calls, but a place to start might again be London Recumbents (see above, or in Dulwich Park on 020 299 6636).

Being a description in brief of how the Sport of Polo, much beloved of Gentlemen has been adapted to be enjoyed by the employment of that marvel of the Modern age

THE BICYCLE

BIKE POLO

WHERE   *Hurlingham Park, Fulham, London*

WHAT   *Informal bicycle polo matches each Wednesday night in summer*

WHY   *Fun, sociable, horses not required*

HOW   *Just turn up with or without bike; 2km from Putney station*

Polo, the sport of kings, has yet to gain a grass-roots following in the comprehensives. It's conceivable that money may be a contributory factor: membership of the Guards Polo Club at Windsor involves a £15,000 joining fee and £5,000 annual subscription, plus there's maintenance for the polo ponies at about twenty grand a year each.

Just like polo, only without the horses. Somewhat cheaper, too

For those of us in the bottom ninety-nine-point-nine per cent of the social heap, there's an affordable and accessible alternative: bicycle polo, which is essentially the same game but without the horses and the platinum credit card.

Bicycle polo is a minority sport, and as with many minority sports, this can be a big advantage. Show some aptitude for it, or at least offer to drive the minibus, and you could find yourself playing in internationals before the year is out.

But it's very enjoyable, participating in sociable two-wheel sport. Some genuine polo players play to their mallet hand in; others are cyclists after some fresh air and a bit of a spin, either as a complement, or an alternative, to road racing or time trialling.

■ Chelsea at home

To go and watch or take part (or hedge your bets and decide when you get there) go to Fulham any Wednesday summer evening when it's not raining too much. In Hurlingham Park in west London, by the north bank of the Thames, the Chelsea Pedallers will do their stuff from about 7pm until dusk.

Shorts are advisable, but you don't need any particular kit, just something comfy that you don't mind getting a bit muddy. Simply turn up and wander round the various games of football, touch rugby and tennis that are taking place elsewhere round the park until you find the bike polo players. They'll probably be on the east side.

You can use your own bike or borrow one of the club's. There's a variety of polo bikes, from BMX adaptations to conventionally sized machines, but the most interesting are old Indian models specially built for polo. Dating from the 1930s, they are fixed-wheel machines (so no brake cables to snag) with sawn-off handlebars, that are especially short on the right-hand side so as not to encumber the mallet. Riding, twirling a mallet at the same time, making contact with the ball and not falling off, takes a bit of getting used to; but is great fun.

Bicycle polo comes in a number of versions. At Hurlingham Park it involves a rugby pitch and posts, teams of four a side, and a soft ball the size of a very large grapefruit, and to score a goal, you have to have both feet on the pedals.

■ Ale fellows well met

When it gets dark everyone decamps to the pub. The cost of an evening's bicycle polo, therefore – a couple of quid sub towards bike upkeep, and maybe a drink or two after – compares favourably to the blank cheques required for the conventional game. The chaps who play here are a friendly bunch, and participation is recommended.

For details, email Tim Dobson

(timd@rolemodelworld.com) or just turn up and get chatting. Bicycle polo can be a gateway to international athlete status: the Chelsea team have been to Scotland and France compete.

An Irishman called Richard Mecredy is credited with devising bicycle polo in 1891. The pitch is officially 150m by 100m and a proper match lasts four chukkas of seven and a half minutes. A side consists of six players, four of whom are on the field at a time. Mixed teams are allowed. Leading international sides are the US, Canada, France, Pakistan and India, where the game is very popular. It is played less formally but enthusiastically in another dozen or so countries, including England. The governing body for polo is the Hurlingham Polo Association, but they're based in Oxfordshire, not in the park.

Roberts of Croydon hand-build specialised polo bicycles, if the game uncovers a passion and your new status as budding international sports star demands a purpose-built bike. www.robertscycles.com. This will have the requisite short handlebars, straight forks, fixed wheel, quick-acceleration gearing, rubber pedals, short wheelbase, and densely-spoked wheels to stop the ball getting lodged inside.

the chaps who play here are a friendly bunch, and participation is recommended

■ Also in the area...

Hurlingham Park is on the Thames Path. The bit of the Thames Path round here, though – roughly between Vauxhall Bridge and Putney Bridge – isn't much on the river and is a bit dull. East from Vauxhall is holiday-snap territory, taking in all the South Bank sights, from the Houses of Parliament to the Eye to Tower Bridge *(see pages 54-61)*. West from Putney is lovely, getting steadily more well-to-do and Henleyesque; passing Richmond and Kingston, Hampton Court, and on through Slough eventually to Windsor and the Great Park.

The River Wandle pours into the Thames from the south bank, right opposite Hurlingham Park. It's a smallish river but has a cycle trail, the 20km Wandle Trail, forming a green corridor from Carshalton up to the Thames. It makes a very pleasant half-day ride (see www.wandle-trail.org for details and a free map).

From London, the best way to get to and from the park is by bike; cycling home on a summer night past a twinkling Hammersmith Bridge after a game and a pint or two is pleasant enough in itself. Most of the chaps who come to play in Hurlingham Park do it by bike, and not for economic reasons.

Over Putney Bridge from the polo, on the south bank, is Barnes Wetland Centre, which offers the

unusual experience of remote-mudflats-birdwatching in London. But the really odd stuff happens west along the Thames path by Kew Gardens, another flat traffic-free 16km or so (don't worry, there are trains back if you need one).

Here, squawking in the trees, flocks of green ring-necked parakeets flit greenly from branch to branch. They give the place the dislocating feeling of being under a rainforest canopy. Originally from the Himalayan foothills, so they know about cool climates, the parakeets established their colony here more than 30 years ago.

■ Other places like this

Bicycle polo activity is found in north Kent, in the shape of the Oakenden Pedallers (see their site www.oakendenpedallers.co.uk), in Sussex (www.polo-velo.net/english/contacts/teams.htm) and Scotland (www.scotpolo.org). There may also be some in summer at Herne Hill Velodrome in south London, but last time we investigated, no-one admitted to knowing anything about it.

This book is really supposed to confine its scope to England and Wales, so this is a little off-topic, but we found that bike polo can be an instant introduction to cyclists abroad. San Francisco has bike polo every Tuesday evening from 6pm until dark in Speedway Meadow, Golden Gate Park (off JFK Drive, about 28th Avenue). We rolled up and found a welcome, and after playing, we were invited round to various people's places for lunch and stuff afterwards, and treated like long-term friends. In the hectic pace of Californian life we quite possibly had been.

Snackstop

Picnic. *You'll probably be too busy playing to want to eat, but bring some snacky energy stuff just in case, and plenty of water and soft drinks.*

Bevvy break

Aragon House, New King's Road. *Likely spot for the post-match drinks, a kilometre or so away. Medium-upmarket sort of place with West-London-professionals atmosphere, and your bike will be safely locked up to the raillings outside with the others belonging to your fellow polo cyclists.*

Quirkshop

Jilly Cooper's 1980s bonkfest Polo was a novel set in the highly-sexed world of international polo. We're still waiting for her bicycle polo sequel.

Tourer's tick list

✓ Thames Path
✓ Holland Park
✓ Barnes Wetland Centre
✓ Kew Gardens

OS 176, grid ref TQ 250761
INFO www.bicyclepolo.org
http://en.wikipedia.org/wiki/Cycle_polo

END TO END

WHERE   *Britain, an island off continental Europe*

WHAT   *The length of the world's seventh-largest island, from south-west to north-east extremity: 1500km*

WHY   *Ultimate challenge; getting measure of our island; chance to raise money for charity; self-growth etc*

HOW   *Train to Penzance; cycle to Land's End, then to John O'Groats*

Riding from **Land's End** to **John O'Groats** is the ultimate British biking experience – the cycling equivalent of climbing Everest, singing in Wagner's Ring, or reading James Joyce's Ulysses. Oxygen and sherpas are more or less optional, as are special talents or years of practice, and it's a damn sight easier to finish. Travel the whole of the land, from fractal West Country greenery, to sagging grey estuaries, to Caledonian massifs.

The ultimate UK bike ride: Land's End to John O'Groats

And on occasion get very, very wet. Most people cycle the 1450-odd kilometres from Land's End to John O'Groats in 7–14 days. Two to three weeks is probably the ideal time.

Whoever said it is better to travel hopefully than to arrive never did the End to End. Travelling and connecting with this patchwork country and its people in a way that's impossible from a train or car, things happen for those on the celebrated pilgrimage. People want to talk, buy drinks, open up closed museums, invite you to their houses; scowling officials smile and give a couple of quid to your charity. You're a star.

van full of luggage and spares; or unsupported, where everything is carried on the bike.

Supported is harder to organise. Vans don't come free, the driver will be able to claim favours forever, and there's an extra person to fit into B&Bs – but it makes the cycling, as well as the journeys to and from the start and finish, much easier.

An unsupported ride means that there is no-one else to worry about before or during the trip, and nobody is racking up a life-long beer-ticket. But the weight of panniers doubles in a headwind, and trebles pushing up a Devon hill.

■ Better elate than never

But the arriving at John O'Groat's is the best bit, by miles. The feeling of elation that the Orkneys stir as they appear over the horizon on that final descent to John O'Groats is a memory for life.

It may inspire a lifetime of barroom bragging, but it will also inspire some admiration and sneaking jealousy, because it is still something of an achievement. Around 4,000 cyclists manage the End to End every year, and that's fewer people than get books published, release a rock CD, or appear on reality TV shows.

It isn't neccessary to be especially fit, rich or adventurous. The most difficult part is making the decision. There are two ways to travel: supported, with a friend driving a

■ The route

Upwards is the usual way to go, as the prevailing winds tend to come from the south-west, but there's not much in it. The most popular course is roughly Lands End-Bristol–Welsh border–Carlisle; then either Glasgow or Edinburgh to Inverness; then Wick or Thurso to John O'Groats. There is no 'official route'. The CTC offer three suggestions – main roads, scenic or Youth Hostels – and can supply details along with some accommodation information. The information pack is free to members (£34 per year, with lots of other benefits: 0870 873 0061, or www.ctc.org.uk). Each route is tried and tested, and around 1600km.

The most rewarding and memorable route will be one that you

plan for yourself, especially if you have a theme for your trip. Route-planning is great fun, best done by the fire on a cold dark night with a glass of something inspiring. Link up friends and family; or be more inventive. I did 'local food and drink' (Cornish pasties, Cheddar, Bath buns, Melton Mowbray pork pies, Yorkshire pud, Edinburgh shortbread etc). Other cyclists have done 'cathedrals' (Wells, Coventry, York, Durham). One chap stayed only at pubs called the Red Lion, and still managed pub-crawls.

There are limitless possiblities. Just avoid A roads whenever you possibly can.

■ Reasons to rail

Penzance is the nearest railway station to Land's End, a fairly hilly ten miles or so away. Land's End itself is a naff theme park; cars pay to get in but bicycles don't have to. There's a finger post (a picture will cost you) and a 'museum'.

John O'Groats is little more than a cluster of souvenir shops, a hotel or two and another finger post photo-op. The nearest stations are both about 30km away, at Thurso and Wick. Taking bikes by train in Scotland can be trying, so check ScotRail's website beforehand.

When's the best time? August is tourist season, which means B&Bs and hostels will be squeezed, so that's best avoided. May to July is the best time for daylight — up till 10 o'clock and even later in Scotland — leaving the options to sit out a rainstorm, say, or return to the road after dinner.

■ Training? Forget it!

Anyone who can make it to work can make it to John O'Groats in three weeks. That 1500km works out at less than 80km a day. Averaging a stately 15kph, that's only five hours' pedalling. (Keen cyclists would almost double that.) Along the way, your fitness will develop, just remember to wind down gradually after the trip with progressively shorter distances. Your thighs will turn to plasticine if you stop cycling abruptly.

Accommodation is the biggest problem. Camping is fun, relatively cheap and flexible. And wet, and heavy. Even a lightweight tent and sleeping gear is a pain to lug around. At £10 per campsite it's not cheap either.

Outside the school holidays, bed & breakfast rooms are easily had. They're £25–£30 per person, typically, and offer privacy, a colour telly, and unlimited copies of old Reader's Digests. If there's no Tourist Info open then ask in a pub, or watch out for 'vacancy' boards on the roads into and out of towns. In high season, a place that's full will usually recommend

Just avoid A roads as much as possible

another, and even phone to help.

Of course, you'll have mined your address book for every friend and relative with a spare room en route where you can stay.

Travel light. Work out the very minimum amount of luggage, and the very maximum cash. Then halve the first and double the second. Two panniers is enough. All you need are a few basic tools and two spare inner Tubes; one set of waterproof wearable everything; two sets of clothes and some hand-wash; a road atlas; a digital camera with a spare memory card; and a very full wallet. Anything else you can buy on the way. In an emergency you won't be more than 20 miles from a bike shop.

As for maps, a two-quid road atlas from a remaindered bookshop will do fine. Tear out pages and fold them up into your map pocket, then chuck the finished pages out along the way.

Whatever route you choose, it'll be the rainiest month since 1836. The wind will make you wish you'd gone the other way, and a lorry will try to run you off the A30. It's just par for a long course.

England is hilly, but if you have to get off and push, well, that's a good way of avoiding saddle soreness. The long slow grinds (Shap Fell, the A9 out of Pitlochry) are notorious. Those oscilloscope-trace Devonian hills are worse. Road signs will habitually lie. The first says Padstow 5; you cycle 20 minutes; the next sign says Padstow 412; you cycle 20 more minutes; the next sign says Padstow 5.

With more than two weeks to hand and a bike with more than ten gears, it's not an exercise of fitness so much as one of patience and budget. The route becomes a succession of rewards: a drink of water at the top of the hill; a cream tea at the next town; a drink or two over dinner in the evening.

The experience will be unique to you. You will always treasure that last mile and cherish every day of the trip. Except for the one with the lorry on the A30.

eye**Sight**

Our greatest fear is not that we are inadequate, our greatest fear is that we are powerful beyond measure. By shining your light, you subconsciously give permission to others to shine theirs.'
Nelson Mandela

Travel can be a liberating experience. As it was for me in 1990, when I was just one hundred yards from Nelson Mandela as he was released from prison. I watched this monumental occasion from on top of a traffic light, amidst a sea of enthralled onlookers.

This was the 'green light' moment that inspired the creation of Eye Books. From the chaos of that day arose an appreciation of the opportunities that the world around us offers, and the desire within me to shine a light for those whose reaction to opportunity is 'can't and don't'.

Our world has been built on dreams, but the drive is often diluted by the corporate and commercial interests offering to live those dreams for us, through celebrity culture and the increasing mechanisation and automation of our lives. Inspiration comes now from those who live outside our daily routines, from those who challenge the way we see things.

Eye Books was born to tell the stories of 'ordinary' people doing 'extraordinary' things. With no experience of publishing, or the constraints that the book 'industry' imposes, Eye Books created a genre of publishing to champion those who live out their dreams.

Ten years on, and sixty stories later, Eye Books has the same ethos. We believe that ethical publishing matters. It is not about just trying to make a quick hit, it is about publishing the stories that affect our lives and the lives of others positively. We publish the books we believe will shine a light on the lives of some and enlighten the lives of many for years to come.

Join us in the community of Eye Books, and share the power these stories evoke.
Dan Hiscocks
Founder and Publisher

eye books

At Eye Books we are constantly challenging the way we see things and do things. But we cannot do this alone. To that end we have created an online club, a community, where members can inspire and be inspired, share knowledge and exchange ideas.

eye**Community**

Membership is free, and you can join by visiting www.eye-books.com, where you will be able to find:

What we publish
Books that truly inspire, by people who have given their all, triumphed over adversity, lived their lives to the full.
Visit the dedicated microsites we have for each of our books online.

Why we publish
To champion those 'ordinary' people doing extraordinary things. The real celebrities of our world who tell stories that celebrate life to the full, not just for 15 minutes.
Books where fact is more compelling than fiction.

How we publish
Eye Books is committed to ethical publishing. Many of our books feature and campaign for various good causes and charities.
We try to minimise our carbon footprint in the manufacturing and distribution of our books.

Who we publish
Many, indeed most of our authors have never written a book before. Many start as readers and club members. If you feel strongly that you have a book in you, and it is a book that is experience driven, inspirational and life affirming, visit the 'How to Become an Author' page on our website. We are always open to new authors.

Eye-Books.com Club is an ever evolving community, as it should be, and benefits from all that our members contribute.

eye-**Books Club** membership offers you:

eye-**News** – a regular emailed newsletter of events in our community.

Special offers and discounts on the books we publish.

Invitations to book launches, signings and author talks.

Correspond with Eye Books authors, directly. About writing, about their books, or about trips you may be planning.

Each month, we receive enquiries from people who have read our books, entered our competitions or heard of us through the media or from friends, people who have a common desire – to make a difference with their lives, however big or small, and to extend the boundaries of everyday life and to learn from others' experiences.

The Eye Books Club is here to support our members, and we want to encourage you to participate. As we all know, the more you put into life, the more you get out of it.

Eye Books membership is free, and it's easy to sign up. Visit our website. Registration takes less than a minute.

eyeBookshelf

THE AMERICAS / ASIA

	The Good Life — Dorian Amos	The Good Life Gets Better — Dorian Amos	Cry From the Highest Mountain — Tess Burrows	Riding the Outlaw Trail — Simon Casson & Richard Adamson	Trail of Visions Route 2 — Vicki Couchman	Riding with Ghosts — Gwen Maka	South of the Border — Gwen Maka	Lost Lands Forgotten Stories — Alexandra Pratt	Frigid Women — Sue and Victoria Riches	Touching Tibet — Niema Ash	First Contact — Mark Anstice	Tea for Two — Polly Benge
eyeThinker	•	•	•			•		•	•		•	•
eyeAdventurer	•	•		•		•	•	•	•		•	•
eyeQuirky					•							
eyeCyclist						•	•					•
eyeRambler												
eyeGift					•							
eyeSpiritual												

AFRICA / EUROPE

	Green Oranges on Lion Mountain — Emily Joy	Zohra's Ladder — Pamela Windo	Walking Away — Charlotte Metcalf	Changing the World One Step at a Time — Michael Meegan	All Will Be Well — Michael Meegan	Seeking Sanctuary — Hilda Reilly	Crap Cycle Lanes — Captain Yellowjersey	50 Quirky Bike Rides...in England and Wales — Rob Ainsley	On the Wall with Hadrian — Bob Bibby	Special Offa — Bob Bibby	The European Job — Jonathan Booth	Fateful Beauty — Natalie Hodgson
eyeThinker	•		•	•	•	•						
eyeAdventurer	•								•		•	•
eyeQuirky								•			•	•
eyeCyclist							•	•				
eyeRambler									•	•		
eyeGift								•				
eyeSpiritual					•	•						

eyeBookshelf

ASIA / AUS

Book	eyeThinker	eyeAdventurer	eyeQuirky	eyeCyclist	eyeRambler	eyeGift	eyeSpiritual
Trail of Visions — *Vicki Couchman*	•	•				•	
Desert Governess — *Phyllis Ellis*	•	•	•				
Fever Tress of Borneo — *Mark Everleigh*							
My Journey with a Remarkable Tree — *Ken Finn*	•	•					
The Jungle Beat — *Roy Follows*	•	•					
Siberian Dreams — *Andy Home*	•	•					
Behind the Veil — *Lydia Laube*	•	•					
Good Morning Afghanistan — *Waseem Mahmood*	•	•					
Jasmine and Arnica — *Nicola Naylor*	•	•					
Prickly Pears of Palestine — *Hilda Reilly*	•						
Last of the Nomads — *W J Peasley*	•	•					
Travels in Outback Australia — *Andrew Stevenson*	•						

EUROPE / CROSS CONTINENT

Book	eyeThinker	eyeAdventurer	eyeQuirky	eyeCyclist	eyeRambler	eyeGift	eyeSpiritual
Con Artist Handbook — *Joel Levy*	•		•			•	
Forensics Handbook — *Pete Moore*	•		•				
Travels with my Daughter — *Niema Ash*	•	•	•			•	
Around the World with 1000 Birds — *Russell Boyman*		•					
Death — *Herbie Brennan*	•	•	•	•		•	•
Discovery Road — *Tim Garratt and Andy Brown*	•						
Great Sects — *Adam Hume Kelly*	•	•	•			•	
Triumph Around the World — *Robbie Marshall*		•					
Blood Sweat and Charity — *Nick Stanhope*							
Traveller's Tales from Heaven and Hell — *Various*			•			•	
Further Traveller's Tales from Heaven and Hell — *Various*			•			•	
More Traveller's Tales from Heaven and Hell — *Various*			•			•	

eye**Bookshelf**

Moods of Future Joys

£7.99

Alastair Humphreys' round the world journey of 46,000 miles was an old-fashioned adventure: long, lonely, low-budget and spontaneous.

This first part of the ride crosses the Middle East and Africa, and continues towards Cape Town. The epic journey succeeded through Humphreys' trust in the kindness of strangers, at a time when the global community was more confused and troubled than ever.

Discovery Road

£9.99
The first people to mountain bike around the world. It is a fast moving inspirational tale of self discovery: full of adventure, conflict, humour, danger and a multitude of colourful characters. Much more than a travelogue, it proves that ordinary people can chase great dreams.

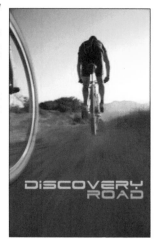

Crap Cycle Lanes

£4.99
Probably the worst bike lanes in the world
(Well, the UK, at any rate), exposed in full colour.
Offences from all over England and Wales.

"So funny, I nearly bought a round"
– A Bloke

*"I'm convinced that it's a real contribution to road
safety"*
– J Stalker

"You'll be hearing from my lawyers"
– K Livingstone

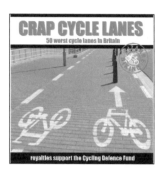

Thunder & Sunshine

£7.99
Following on from his first best-seller, Alastair
leaves Cape Town wondering whether he will
ever make it home. As he sets sail from South
Africa, he has more than three quarters of the
way left to go. Up through the America's,
Canada and Alaska before crossing into Asia,
riding through Russia, Siberia and back
through Europe. A truly carbon neutral book.

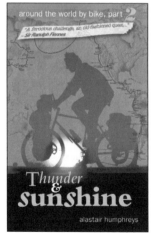

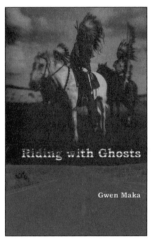

Riding With Ghosts

£7.99
An interest in Native American Indian history and a desire to push herself to the limits sees Gwen (a solo woman) try to bicycle the trail from Seattle to Mexico. Her frank and outrageous account is shared an involvement with the West and it's pioneering past. We almost catch a glimpse of Crazy Horse.

Blood Sweat & Charity

£9.99
The only charity challenge guidebook to help you through any or all of the process; from identifying the challenge or the cause, to how to document it and maximise the fundraising and awareness along with making sure that you are physically prepared for whatever you take on.

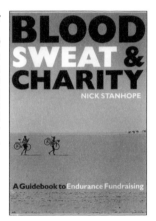

Riding with Ghosts
– South of the border

£7.99
Having ridden, saddle sore, from Seattle
to Mexico, Gwen continued down the
America's to San Jose in Costa Rica.
She finds interest in all the pioneers of
the South ~ Columbus, Cortes and
Montezuma.
She still journeys with abandon and gives
the reader a blend of courage, candour
and humour.

Tea for two

£7.99
Tim and Polly head to war-torn Assam
and follow the 400 mile route taken to
enlightenment by the Buddha. The
Buddha took 6 years. They had 6 weeks
and two bicycles. They hoped, if they
could dodge the civil war around them,
their love would stand the strain.

A true love story and a great read.